"Peter often gets a bad rap in evangelical circles. He denied Christ three times. Paul publicly rebuked him. But Jesus loved him and named him *Rocky*—loyal, steadfast, the leader of the early church, and willing to die for Christ (which he ultimately did). Read this wonderfully encouraging portrait of Peter (there aren't many of them in print!), and let it challenge you to be bold for Christ."

—Dr. William B. Barcley
Senior Pastor, Sovereign Grace Presbyterian Church
Adjunct Professor, Reformed Theological Seminary
Charlotte, N.C.

"Readers familiar with Dr. Thomas' work will open this book and smile— here is the familiar pastoral touch, compact but penetrating exposition, and trademark application we have come to relish from his pen, applied to the life of Peter. If you struggle, if you fail, if you wonder if the good news is really good, let this work give you fresh hope from Peter's example. Far from simply recounting the facts and failures of Peter's life, Dr. Thomas gives us a page-turning biography of the Apostle with whom we identify so easily, but with details and insights we overlook so frequently."

—Dr. Gabriel N.E. Fluhrer
Senior Pastor, First Presbyterian Church
Chattanooga, Tenn.

"It is easy to identify with Simon Peter, and many of us do. He is a rock that crumbled and yet under God opened the kingdom of God to the nations. His flaws and failures are obvious, and yet they cannot overshadow the transforming power of Christ in his life. Peter's story gives us hope, and no one retells it better than Derek Thomas. Here, in chapter after chapter, he helps us to 'shadow' Peter. As we do so, we learn the ways of the Master alongside Peter. More than that, our love for the Master grows as we witness the constancy and strength of His love and prayers. In page after page, Dr. Thomas introduces us to the Savior who is the same in our 'today' as He was 'yesterday' in His life-re-shaping ministry to Simon Peter. Perhaps not every Christian book needs to be enjoyable to be helpful, but this one is both!"

—Dr. Sinclair B. Ferguson
Chancellor's Professor of Systematic Theology,
Reformed Theological Seminary
Teaching Fellow, Ligonier Ministries

"The life of Peter was tumultuous, with highs and lows, triumphs and defeats, reminding us of our own victories and defeats. Derek Thomas, who is well known for his powerful preaching, guides us through Peter's life in this wonderful book. As readers we are convicted, comforted, and challenged by the life of Peter as recorded in the Word of God."

—DR. THOMAS R. SCHREINER
James Buchanan Harrison Professor of New Testament Interpretation
The Southern Baptist Theological Seminary
Louisville, Ky.

The Life of Peter

The Life of Peter

Molded in the Master's Hands

DEREK W.H. THOMAS

 LIGONIER MINISTRIES

The Life of Peter: Molded in the Master's Hands
© 2024 by Derek W.H. Thomas

Published by Ligonier Ministries
421 Ligonier Court, Sanford, FL 32771
Ligonier.org

Printed in China
Amity Printing Company
0000524
First printing

ISBN 978-1-64289-608-4 (Hardcover)
ISBN 978-1-64289-609-1 (ePub)

Cover design: Ligonier Creative
Interior design and typeset: Katherine Lloyd, The DESK

Unless otherwise noted, Scripture quotations are from the ESV® Bible (The Holy Bible, English Standard Version®), copyright © 2001 by Crossway, a publishing ministry of Good News Publishers. Used by permission. All rights reserved.

Scripture quotations marked KJV are from the King James Version. Public domain.

Library of Congress Control Number: 2023945594

Dedicated to

Rev. Dr. Leslie Holmes

Pastor, Theologian, Fellow Presbyter, Friend

"There is a friend who sticks closer than a brother."

Proverbs 18:24

Contents

Acknowledgments

I have many people to thank, not least the members of First Presbyterian Church, Columbia, S.C., whose support and love I have known for over a decade. Then there is the session of First Presbyterian Church, who kindly gave me a two-month sabbatical in the summer of 2022 to write this book. The change of rhythm proved delightful. Ligonier Ministries and its vice president of publishing, Thomas Brewer, were kind enough to consider publishing this book. Debbie Thompson and Grayson Lambert both read and corrected the manuscript, and I cannot thank them enough for their insights. What errors remain are mine. About halfway through the writing, Mac and Mary McFadden kindly offered us a few days in their wonderful beach home. It was a haven, and a big thank-you is in order!

Certainly not least, I thank my wife of forty-six years, Rosemary. She suffers long with my absences in the study even during a two-month sabbatical.

Finally, I want to thank one more person for the encouragement he provided me over the last few years. This book would not have been written without his brotherly love and support. Dr. Leslie Holmes hails from Belfast, Northern Ireland, where I first met him more than four decades ago. This book is dedicated to you, dear brother. Thank you for being "a friend who sticks closer than a brother" (Prov. 18:24).

Introduction

Peter has been overshadowed by Paul. As just one example, open the New Testament. In terms of location, Peter's two epistles in the canon of Scripture are eclipsed by the many letters of Paul.

But it was to Peter, not Paul, that Jesus made the promise that the New Testament church would be built, in human terms, on his contribution. Playing on the similar Greek words for "Peter" and "rock," Jesus told him, "You are Peter, and on this rock I will build my church, and the gates of hell shall not prevail against it" (Matt. 16:18). That statement alone sets Peter apart from all the other Apostles.

Peter, along with his brother Andrew, was the first disciple Jesus called. Whereas we know very little about some of the disciples, Peter appears prominently throughout the Gospels. Peter's life is told, warts and all. The highs and lows (and there are two significant and troubling lows) make his life something of a roller-coaster ride.

He was a fisherman in Galilee, along with his brother and the Sons of Thunder, James and John. Though they never went to anything like a modern university, their synagogue studies, deeply rooted in the study of the Old Testament, made them well schooled in Scripture and the fundamentals of a basic education.

Peter's personality was dynamic. He was enthusiastic, erratic, and excitable, and he often spoke before he thought. He loved Jesus the moment he saw Him, and he was capable of great loyalty. But he was also headstrong and sometimes questioned his Master, though always out of love. One gets the impression (reading Acts, for example) that Paul could do no wrong. Paul was probably difficult to work for and with. His was a type A personality that didn't suffer fools gladly. But Peter was different—very different.

Paintings of Peter abound. The one by Peter Paul Rubens (1577–1640), painted roughly during the time of the Synod of Dort in 1618, shows Peter as an older man, in his sixties, shortly before his death. Looking off to the right, he is wearing a golden cloak. He looks to be a large man, portly, with gray hair, thinning on top, and a full gray-and-white beard. His eyes are looking upward, and his face is lean and chiseled. His hands are large, and in his right hand he holds two large keys, one gold and one silver. It is a stunning portrait, an artist's impression of what Peter might have looked like. But the painting evokes a man of resolve *and* tenderness. A kind and gentle person, someone you could easily talk to.

In this book, we will examine Peter's life from the accounts of the Gospels and Acts. Occasionally, we will draw from his two epistles lessons that Peter may have learned during his life with Jesus and the early days of the church and pondered in the decades that followed. There are gaps: after Acts 15, we hear no more about Peter. An earlier rift seemed to have developed between Peter and Paul after a blistering episode in the church at Antioch that Paul all too vividly recounts in Galatians 2 and that Peter undoubtedly read. There are further references to Peter in 1 Corinthians, suggesting that he was in Corinth for a season. But then, nothing, until he reappears in Rome, where he and his wife (as well as Paul) are executed at the hands of Emperor Nero. None of these events in Rome are to be found in Scripture, but the historical tradition seems sound. There is a reference in 1 Peter 5:13 of Peter's writing from "Babylon," a euphemism suggesting that he was in Rome.

There are, of course, Roman Catholic claims about the primacy of Peter, insisting that he was the first pope in Rome and that God established an Apostolic succession as primacy over the church was passed from one pope to the next. But these claims were made after Peter was dead, and Scripture gives no hint of them.

I hope this brief account of Peter's life will prove helpful. Its first appearance was as a series of sermons delivered at First Presbyterian Church in Columbia, S.C. The second outing came by way of shortened, twenty-minute DVDs recorded for Ligonier Ministries. The third iteration is this book, expanded and changed to reflect the difference between the written and spoken word. Enjoy.

—Derek W.H. Thomas
Summer 2022

1

What Is Your Name?

Do you ever wonder what it would be like to meet Jesus in person? Every Christian does. All kinds of questions run through your head:

What does He look like?
How tall is He?
What does His voice sound like?

Peter knew the answers to these questions. Meeting Jesus was a life-changing moment for him.

Paintings of Peter show him as an older man, full-figured and slightly balding. There exists to this day, in the catacombs in Rome, a graffito with the name PETRUS in bold red. Rome is where Peter was crucified at the hands of Emperor Nero in AD 64. But Peter first encountered Jesus more than thirty years earlier. As we meet him for the first time in John's gospel (John 1:35–42), he was probably around thirty years old, roughly the same age as Jesus.

Peter and his brother Andrew, along with the two brothers James and John (elsewhere known as Boanerges, or Sons of Thunder, a nickname given to them by Jesus because of their committed preaching; Mark 3:17), had an established fishing business in Bethsaida, Galilee (John 1:44). Bethsaida had been raised to the status of a city by the infamous Philip the Tetrarch, who later married the equally infamous Salome, the one who asked for the head of John the Baptist on a plate.

Peter was a fisherman. Scholars often doubt that Peter could write the complex Greek of the epistle known as 2 Peter. But Bethsaida was a thoroughly

Hellenistic city. Peter would have been taught Hebrew, Aramaic, and Greek, as well as possibly some Latin, in the established synagogue education system. Even today, lack of a formal education doesn't mean that someone is uneducated. I have known many who never went to college whose language skills and knowledge of Scripture were profound. My late mother left school at sixteen to care for her ailing father, but she could hold her own on literature and music. Just because Peter and some of the other disciples earned their living fishing the Sea of Galilee does not mean that they were poorly educated.

Peter's Aramaic name was *Simōn* and denoted the idea of "obedient." Transliterated into Greek, it became *Symeon*. Jesus called him "Peter" (initially at the time of his calling as a disciple [John 1:42] and later reaffirmed at Caesarea Philippi [Matt. 16:18]) because He either saw something in him or desired something from him. The name means "rock" or "stone." Its Aramaic equivalent was *Kephas* (its English cognate is *Cephas*). "Andrew," the name of Peter's brother, is an entirely Greek name, indicating some degree of Hellenization (Greek cultural influence) on the part of their parents.

But something had happened that had taken Andrew and Peter down south to Bethany, on the eastern side of the river Jordan. An extraordinary preacher had emerged by the name of John the Baptist. Huge crowds were going into the countryside to hear him preach and receive the baptism of repentance he offered.

Priests and Levites were sent from Jerusalem to inquire about his identity (John 1:19). Some wondered whether he might be the long-awaited Messiah, the One prophesied in the Scriptures who would deliver the people of Israel from their sins. But he was not (v. 20). Neither was he Elijah. Since the prophet Elijah had not died but instead been taken into heaven alive, a belief emerged among Second Temple Jews that he might return one day. An empty seat was kept for him in Jewish homes at the celebration of Passover.

John was none of these. Instead, he identified himself as the one depicted by the prophet Isaiah as "the voice of one crying out in the wilderness, 'Make straight the way of the Lord'" (John 1:23, quoting Isa. 40:3). Furthermore, John the Baptist pointed to another, One who stood among them, "the strap of whose sandal [he was] not worthy to untie" (John 1:27). He was referring to Jesus, who had also come down from Galilee to hear His cousin preaching in the wilderness.

John the Baptist was the forerunner, the one who prepared the way for

Jesus' ministry. He preached a message of repentance, calling Israel to turn from its sins, and offered a baptism of repentance in the Jordan River. On this occasion, Jesus was there and asking for baptism. After John identified Him as "the Lamb of God, who takes away the sin of the world!" (John 1:29), something extraordinary happened: the Spirit descended on Jesus in the form of a dove (v. 32). "And I have seen and have borne witness that this is the Son of God," John declared (v. 34). And elsewhere, we read that a voice was heard from heaven: "You are my beloved Son; with you I am well pleased" (Mark 1:11).

Why was it necessary for Jesus, the sinless Lamb of God, to receive a baptism of repentance? Why should He undergo this water ordeal of judgment? The answer is *substitution*. He was identifying Himself with our sin. Even the Baptist balked, protesting, "I need to be baptized by you, and do you come to me?" (Matt. 3:14). But it was for this reason that Jesus had come: to provide a way back from the wilderness to Eden. "For our sake he made him to be sin who knew no sin, so that in him we might become the righteousness of God" (2 Cor. 5:21).

The long-awaited Messiah had come!

An Eyewitness of Jesus

Peter came to Bethsaida to see and hear John the Baptist. But he did not know that God had other plans for him, plans that would change his life completely.

It was the day after Jesus' baptism. Andrew and an unnamed disciple, probably John (John 1:35, 40), overheard the Baptist refer to Jesus as "the Lamb of God" (v. 36). The expression would have evoked powerful images in the minds of devout Jews. They would have recalled the incident with Abraham when a ram was caught in the thicket by its horns and the sacrifice of Isaac was averted (Gen. 22:1–24). They would have remembered the annual ritual of sacrificing a lamb for Passover (Ex. 12:43–51). And they would have recollected that the prophet Isaiah, in the fourth Servant Song, referred to "a lamb that is led to the slaughter" (Isa. 53:7).

There is always something about Jesus that entices and attracts attention. Andrew was bold enough to ask where Jesus was staying (the account in John covers several days, and Jesus would have needed somewhere to eat and sleep [cf. John 1:29, 35, 43]). We are not told who these hospitable folks were, but imagine the stories they could relate in later years about Jesus' having slept in their house!

Before leaving for the place where Jesus was staying, Andrew did something significant that had consequences. He went and found his brother Simon and brought him to meet Jesus. This may well have been the most important thing Andrew ever did! On one level, this is a small matter. It is perfectly understandable that a brother might want his sibling to experience meeting Jesus for the first time. But on another level, we never know when small things will end up having significant outcomes. God is in the details.

John, the gospel author, is recalling a day when he and Peter, along with many others, saw Jesus for the first time. They were eyewitnesses. John is writing not about myths and fables but about actual historical acts that he witnessed with his own eyes. The Apostles were eyewitnesses. Later, after the betrayal of Judas, Luke records that Judas' replacement as one of the twelve Apostles must be "a witness to [Jesus'] resurrection" (Acts 1:22).

Scholars sometimes scoff at the reliability of eyewitness recollections, particularly after many years have passed. In today's legal system, testimonies often reveal wide-ranging recollections of past events, giving eyewitness accounts little credibility. But recent scholarship has demonstrated that when issues of deep religious significance are witnessed, the story is recalled over and over and embedded in the mind with accurate details.[1] John is recalling his own first meeting with Jesus, and he remembers places and conversations and the passing of days ("the next day" [John 1:29, 35, 43]). Peter would later recall Jesus' transfiguration and write, "We were eyewitnesses of his majesty" (2 Peter 1:16). Peter wanted us to know that he was there when it happened. "I saw it with my own eyes!"

And for Peter, having these eyewitness accounts written down in Scripture was even more important. Why? Because "no prophecy was ever produced by the will of man, but men spoke from God as they were carried along by the Holy Spirit" (2 Peter 1:21). The Bible is the infallible, inerrant Word of God. Its testimony is true and can be relied on. It is the source of all wisdom, in every circumstance of life.

A Seeker, but of Whom?

Initially, Peter was a seeker of John the Baptist. Intrigued by the news that had reached Galilee about a rather strange figure who was clothed in camel's hair and eating locusts and wild honey and who had appeared out of nowhere, one who reminded people of the prophet Elijah, Peter, joined by the rest of his fishing company, went south to meet this new figure. The outcome of this journey proved very different from what he might initially have expected: Peter not only met John the Baptist but also met the Messiah!

Peter had been a student of the Scriptures since he was a small boy. He knew the Scripture that spoke of the "offspring" of the woman (Gen. 3:15), the prophet like Moses (Deut. 18:18), the King like David who would "establish the throne of his kingdom forever" (2 Sam. 7:13), and the Suffering Servant who would bear "the sin of many" (Isa. 53:12). And now Peter saw the fulfillment of these prophecies. The Messiah was here.

The promised Messiah, the One whom Peter will later confess as "the Christ" (Matt. 16:16), was standing before him *in the flesh*! "We have found the Messiah," Andrew told his brother, and John, recalling the incident, translates it in parentheses as "Christ" for his Hellenistic readers (John 1:41). Peter had been brought to see Jesus by his brother Andrew, and both brothers were invited to spend the day at the place where Jesus was lodging that week. Intrigue drew them to Bethsaida, but they did not yet know that in God's providence, greater things were planned for them. Roughly contemporaries, Jesus and Peter had been raised less than twenty miles apart, but they had apparently never met. In those silent years of preparation, Jesus kept His identity a close secret. But on this day, His identity was a matter of public record. Peter came face-to-face with Jesus and became a disciple.

It is not important that we know the exact day on which we became disciples. Some are brought to Christ as a mother greets her sleeping baby—"with a kiss," as the hymn writer Christina Rossetti once said.[2] Some come to faith before they are ever conscious and only later express their faith. But some, like me, can recall the actual day (and even time) that they first came to believe in Jesus Christ and celebrate it every year thereafter. What is crucial is that we find Jesus and, when we do, that we believe in Him. Without Him, we are lost. When we find Him, we also find ourselves. With Jesus, life takes on an entirely new meaning and purpose.

A New Name

Our names are important to us. I have three names, two of which are my two grandfathers' names. It has made me think of them almost every day, particularly when one of them died when I was seven. I can recall details of events and conversations I shared with both and a message that one gave me a week before he died of cancer. And what was that message, you ask? He gave me a green Parker fountain pen and told me to write a book!

We read that when Andrew brought Peter to Jesus, He looked at him and said: "You are Simon the son of John. You shall be called Cephas" (John 1:42). As we have already noted, *Cephas* and "Peter" are from the Aramaic and Greek words for "rock" or "stone." John, the author of the gospel, translates *Cephas* as "Peter" for his Greek readers. In making this statement, Jesus anticipates an event that would be hardly fathomable for Peter at this moment. It would take place way up north, at Caesarea Philippi, in the foothills of Mount Hermon, when Jesus would tell Peter, "You are Peter, and on this rock I will build my church, and the gates of hell shall not prevail against it" (Matt. 16:18). The Greek is a play on the name "Peter" (*petros*) and the word "rock" (*petra*). We will examine this incident in greater detail later, but on his very first encounter with Jesus, Peter was to be known as Rocky. He had a part to play in the emerging, fledgling church that would be of immense significance. After all, when you read the first twelve chapters of Acts, the account is almost entirely about Peter.

Having one's name changed is deeply significant in Scripture. Think of Abram/Abraham, Jacob/Israel, and Gideon/Jerubbaal, for example (Gen. 17:5; 35:10; Judg. 6:32). Each one was pivotal in the shaping of redemptive history. Jesus seems to be telling Peter: "I am going to build My church, and you will be important in that story. You will be a foundational rock." Though Peter will stumble, Jesus will restore him so that Peter can play the part destined for him and play it magnificently. John, in telling the story, knows that his readers will already be aware of Peter's threefold denial, but John also realizes that his readers will know of Peter's recovery, too, and depending on when John's gospel was written,[3] they may also be aware that he was crucified in AD 64 at the hands of Emperor Nero. A "rock" indeed!

Humanly speaking, none of this would have been possible had Andrew not searched out his brother in the immense crowds attending John the Baptist's preaching and brought him to meet Jesus. You might have only one significant work to do in your life, and you must make sure that you accomplish it. And what could be more significant than introducing a sibling to Jesus?

Peter has been found, and he has become a disciple of Jesus.

2

A Sinful Man

The world in which we live has almost no concept of sin. People make "mistakes" and are sorry, mostly for the inconvenience that these "mistakes" have on themselves. Confessing sin doesn't come naturally—it doesn't today, and it didn't in Peter's time. In a world where God has been cast aside, there is no sense of holiness by which to measure the offensiveness of sin. Even in the church, God is too often brought down to the measure of man and His holiness is belittled. As David Wells observed:

> It is one of the defining marks of Our Time that God is now weightless. I do not mean by this that he is ethereal but rather that he has become unimportant. He rests upon the world so inconsequentially as not to be noticeable. He has lost his saliency for human life.
>
> Those who assure the pollsters of their belief in God's existence may nonetheless consider him less interesting than television, his commands less authoritative than their appetites for affluence and influence, his judgment no more awe-inspiring than the evening news, and his truth less compelling than the advertisers' sweet fog of flattery and lies. That is weightlessness.[1]

Before Peter can be useful to God, he must come face-to-face with his sin. Before he can appreciate who *Jesus* is, he must appreciate who *Peter* is. Peter must look into the mirror and see the sinner who is staring back at him.

Perhaps several weeks have now passed since Simon Peter's first encounter with Jesus. The disciples have returned to Galilee and, more importantly, to work. Peter, Andrew, James, and John made their living catching and selling fish. After a week or more away from home, it was time to make some money. But Jesus is also in Galilee, healing a man with an unclean demon in the synagogue in Capernaum, on the shore of the Sea of Galilee (Luke 4:31–37). After that, Jesus went to Simon Peter's house and healed his mother-in-law (vv. 38–39). Then Jesus disappeared to "a desolate place" (v. 42), after which He began to preach "the good news of the kingdom of God" in synagogues all over Judea (v. 43).

One interesting fact in Luke's account is that Peter had a mother-in-law and, therefore, a wife (though she is not mentioned). But even putting these pieces together, we still know next to nothing about the private lives of the disciples. How many of the other disciples were married? Sticking with our focus on Peter, Roman Catholicism argues that Peter was not married, partly because of its insistence on the priestly vow of celibacy. After all, it would hardly do for the first pope of Rome to have a wife! Yet Paul in 1 Corinthians 9:4–5 explicitly insists on the right of the Apostles to marry: "Do we not have the right to eat and drink? Do we not have the right to take along a believing wife, as do the other apostles and the brothers of the Lord and Cephas?" Roman Catholics, therefore, have to reinterpret the word "wife."[2]

It is curious why there is no mention of a dutiful daughter sitting by her sick mother's bed. Surely an eyewitness account would not leave that out (Matt. 8:14–15; Luke 4:38–39). Unless, of course, she had already died. But there is strong testimony elsewhere to Peter's wife's being alive, and later in this book, we will relate her death by crucifixion in Rome shortly before Peter's execution. We are not told whether Peter's wife was in the room with her sick mother. The focus is Jesus, not Peter's mother-in-law. The authors of the Gospels were not writing a biography of Peter, as I am attempting to do here.

Futility and Frustration

Ernest Hemingway wrote a book called *The Old Man and the Sea*. It is set in the Gulf of Mexico and tells of a man who has gone fishing. He catches a large marlin, too big to haul into the boat. So he attaches it to the side of the boat. When he finally gets ashore (it took a day), only a skeleton is left. Sharks have eaten the marlin.

The story is a parable. You work hard, and at the end of the day you have nothing to show for it. You save all your life for retirement, denying yourself little luxuries along the way, only to die of a heart attack two months after you retire. Simon Peter could relate to this story that morning when he came back from a night of fishing. He had nothing to show for all his labor.

The four disciples—Peter, Andrew, James, and John, two sets of brothers—are described as business "partners" (Luke 5:10). If they were about thirty years old when they first met Jesus, they would have been fishing these waters for more than a decade. They would have been familiar with local weather patterns, the areas of the lake most conducive to catching fish, and the time of day or night best suited for productive fishing. But for all their knowledge of fishing, the night had been fruitless: they "toiled all night and took nothing!" (v. 5).

Scholars surmise that they used trammel nets, circular nets that needed to be cast in a certain way to allow for the nets to open fully and drop into the water. We catch the four disciples early in the morning on the shore of Lake Gennesaret.[3] There are two boats (one of which Peter owned [v. 3]), and the disciples are in the water, "washing their nets" (v. 2), removing seaweed and other flotsam and jetsam caught in their nets. Given that they were up all night and caught nothing, one has little trouble imagining that they are tired and frustrated.

Jesus is on the shoreline, and a large crowd wants to hear from Him (v. 1). Jesus gets into one of the boats and asks the disciples to place the boat in such a way that He can preach to the crowd, with the sea providing something of an amphitheater effect to amplify His voice. After this is done, Jesus asks Peter to "put out into the deep and let down [his] nets for a catch" (v. 4). You can almost sense the frustration in Peter's response: "Master, we toiled all night and took nothing!" Maybe Peter was thinking: "I just want to go home and sleep a little! You should stick to preaching, and I will stick to fishing!" But obedience gets the better part of him, and he replies, "But at your word I will let down the nets" (v. 5).

Sometimes Jesus may ask of us things that do not make sense *to us*, but they do *to Him*. It is the way of wisdom to do as He says. His own mother had the presence of mind at a wedding in nearby Cana of Galilee, when the wine ran out, to tell the servants, "Do whatever he tells you" (John 2:5). That is always the proper response.

Peter's journey with Jesus was only beginning. He had come to confess that Jesus was the Messiah, but he had not yet seen all that the Messiah could do.[4] Peter had glimpsed it in the way that his mother-in-law was healed. But there was much more for Peter to know about Jesus—so much more. Peter would sense it when he urged his readers in the closing lines of his second epistle to "grow in the grace and knowledge of our Lord and Savior Jesus Christ" (2 Peter 3:18). Growing in Christ begins by listening to Him and obeying everything that He says to you. Again, in Peter's first epistle, he exhorts, "Like newborn infants, long for the pure spiritual milk, that by it you may grow up into salvation" (1 Peter 2:2). That is what Peter is right now, a newborn infant, learning to trust Jesus even when it doesn't make any sense.

A Moment of Fear

Then it happened. A miracle! With so many fish that the nets were breaking, the fishermen shout to some of the folk on the shore to come and help them (Luke 5:6–7). People are throwing fish into the two boats from the nets, and the boats are at the point of sinking. When Jesus performs a miracle, there are no half measures! Something from another realm has perforated into the world of space and time as we know it, and the hand of God is manifest.

Peter senses it. There is so much more to Jesus than he has thought. He is in the presence of something—or really, Some*one*—holy. And by way of contrast, Peter is also aware that he is not. He gets onto his knees in the boat, now full of fish, and pleads, "Depart from me, for I am a sinful man, O Lord" (Luke 5:8). There is something almost comical about it. Half-dead fish are flopping about, the boat is almost at sinking point, but Peter is on his knees, expressing his sin!

When the prophet Isaiah found himself in the temple, in the year that King Uzziah died, he "saw the Lord sitting upon a throne, high and lifted up; and the train of his robe filled the temple" (Isa. 6:1). Seraphim hailed Him, "Holy, holy, holy . . . ; the whole earth is full of his glory!" (v. 3). And Isaiah's response? "Woe is me! For I am lost; for I am a man of unclean lips, and I dwell in the midst of a people of unclean lips; for my eyes have seen the King, the LORD of hosts!" (v. 5). Before the resplendent sight of God's holiness, the prophet (who had the cleanest lips in Israel!) saw himself as unclean. The Apostle John had a similar experience when he saw a vision of the Son of Man in magnificent glory. "I fell at his feet as though dead," he reported (Rev. 1:17). Ezekiel had a similar experience as well (Ezek. 1:28).

Peter could have responded with delight, knowing, perhaps, that he would never be hungry again. He could have thought to himself, "I could become a rich man if I took Jesus with me every time I went fishing." But such thoughts would have been unworthy. Instead, Peter caught a glimpse of his wretchedness. He saw himself as polluted and in need of cleansing.

Jesus had no compulsion to be in the presence of a sinner such as Peter except His love for Peter. He had called Peter to be a believer by acknowledging that Peter was a sinner, desperately in need of a Savior. The good news that Jesus had preached in the boat that morning was that a holy God may stand in the presence of sinners such as Peter who know that forgiveness is possible through faith.

Fishers of Men

"Do not be afraid," Jesus said (Luke 5:10). There are more than three hundred occurrences of "Fear not" or "Do not be afraid" in the Bible. Some scholars suggest, by stretching the phraseology a little, that there might be as many as 365, one for each day of the year. The good news is that we can stand in Jesus' holy presence and not be afraid.

The catch of fish was a parable. Peter has a new job. Though he will return to fishing after Jesus is crucified—an equally fruitless occasion until Jesus arrives, freshly risen from the grave (John 21:1–14)—fishing *fish* was no longer to be his occupation. He was to become a fisher of *men*.

There are sinners to be reached. There is a gospel to be proclaimed. There is a church to be planted in Jesus' name. Peter will be in the vanguard of a host of disciples who must heed Christ's commission: "Go therefore and make disciples of all nations, baptizing them in the name of the Father and of the Son and of the Holy Spirit, teaching them to observe all that I have commanded you. And behold, I am with you always, to the end of the age" (Matt. 28:19–20).

Peter is already a believer, but now he is to be one of Jesus' *disciples*. He has a new calling. He must adjust ties to family and vocation and begin a new life. Simon, along with his brother and the Sons of Thunder, who leave their father, Zebedee, in the boat along with day workers, immediately leaves to follow Jesus (Matt. 4:18–22; Mark 1:16–20; Luke 5:11).

"They left everything and followed him" (Luke 5:11).

Everything!

We are not all called to be disciples in the sense that Peter and the others were, but we are called to put Jesus first in *everything*. Yet if Jesus were to call you to follow Him like Peter, would you? The answer is a measure of our commitment to Him.

Jesus calls us o'er the tumult
    of our life's wild, restless sea;
day by day his voice invites me,
    saying "Christian, follow me!"

As the first disciples heard it
    by the Galilean lake,
turned from home and toil and kindred,
    leaving all for his dear sake.

Jesus calls us from the worship
    of the vain world's golden store,
from each idol that would keep us,
    saying "Christian, love me more."

In our joys and in our sorrows,
    days of toil and hours of ease,
still he calls, in cares and pleasures,
    "Christian, love me more than these."

Jesus calls us! In your mercy,
    Savior, help us hear your call;
give our hearts to your obedience,
    serve and love you best of all![5]

3

Treading Water

In the previous chapter, we left Peter at the miraculous catch of fish. Several months have now passed, possibly a whole year. At some point, Peter witnessed a miracle that Jesus performed: He raised a little girl from the dead (Matt. 9:23–26; Mark 5:37–43; Luke 8:51–56). But Peter also witnessed a great deal more. He heard Jesus proclaim the Sermon on the Mount. He witnessed Jesus cleansing lepers, healing those possessed by demons, and much more.

These were months of watching and listening and growing. There is work for Peter to do, but first he must learn from his Master. He must be assured of his newly found Savior's identity and powers. Before he can be a witness *for* Jesus, he must be a witness *of* Jesus.

A little later, Jesus called the twelve disciples "apostles" (Matt. 10:1–4). Jesus gave them a certain status. Matthew lists them in a specific order, referring to Simon, "who is called Peter," as "first" (v. 2).[1] Jesus saw in Peter leadership potential from the very beginning. Peter was a representative agent for Jesus, proclaiming the kingdom of God.

It is also fascinating that Mark (keep in mind that Mark's gospel is often thought to be Peter's memoirs) tells us that Jesus called the disciples in order "that they might be with him" (Mark 3:14). In Jesus' true humanity, He needed friendship. He desired the company of others, including Peter, as He made His journey to Jerusalem and the cross.

All of Jesus' miracles are spectacular, but some seem even more spectacular than others. Each one is a demonstration of His identity. When John the Baptist was arrested and imprisoned by Herod, he experienced a moment of doubt.

He sent word by his disciples to Jesus to ask, "Are you the one who is to come, or shall we look for another?" (Matt. 11:3). And the reply? A quotation from Isaiah 35:5–6 referring to the miracles that would be associated with the coming of the Messiah. John had no need to doubt. Jesus was the genuine Messiah.

The Apostles repeated some of the miracles they saw Jesus perform. The miracles are later referred to as "signs and wonders and mighty works" (2 Cor. 12:12; cf. Acts 2:22, 43; 4:30; 5:12; 6:8). They were signs in the sense that the miracles pointed to the identity of Jesus and His Apostles. They were wonders because each miracle evoked a sense of awe. And they were mighty acts because they pointed to a supernatural power at work in their midst.

Perhaps no miracle was more spectacular than the one that finds Jesus and Peter walking on the surface of the Sea of Galilee. And the fact that Matthew's account (Matt. 14:22–33) unusually employs the word "immediately" three times (vv. 22, 27, 31)—a stylistic choice more typical of Mark—suggests that Matthew is recording an eyewitness account given to him by Peter himself. Peter is saying to Matthew, "I want you to tell this story as I saw it!"

And what a story it is! A storm at sea. Stunning miracles involving both Jesus and Peter. And an embarrassing collapse of faith followed by a rescuing hand of the Master.

Faith Will Be Tested

The disciples are in a boat on the Sea of Galilee because Jesus told them to "go before him to the other side" (Matt. 14:22). Crowds had gathered to hear Jesus. They wanted to see miracles too. But it was now time to dismiss them because evening was approaching.

The disciples are "a long way from the land" (Matt. 14:24) when a storm arises. This is not the first storm that Peter has witnessed. He had seen Jesus' power in stilling a storm on the Sea of Galilee before (8:23–27).

The Sea of Galilee is 680 feet above sea level, and 30 miles to the north, Mount Hermon rises to an impressive 9,000 feet. Topography dictates that sudden downdrafts of cold air from the north can quickly cause windy gusts and choppy waves on the Sea of Galilee. No doubt the disciples had experienced these many times. Yet on this occasion, they were in trouble at sea because they had obeyed their Master's command to sail to the other side. Obedience can sometimes get you into trouble.

Faith will always be tested. It was one of the very first lessons that the Apostle Paul learned following his first missionary journey: "Through many tribulations we must enter the kingdom of God" (Acts 14:22). Peter would reflect on this idea many times afterward: "Beloved, do not be surprised at the fiery trial when it comes upon you to test you, as though something strange were happening to you. But rejoice insofar as you share Christ's sufferings, that you may also rejoice and be glad when his glory is revealed" (1 Peter 4:12–13). "And after you have suffered a little while, the God of all grace, who has called you to his eternal glory in Christ, will himself restore, confirm, strengthen, and establish you" (5:10).

Peter came to understand all too well that there are "various trials" (1 Peter 1:6). The word translated "various" (Greek, *poikilos*) suggests *multivariate*, an entire rainbow of tribulations: physical, spiritual, mental, or even a combination of all three. They may appear to be strange, and God may orchestrate them for a season, but He is always in control. Still, we need never think that He will abandon us.

> God moves in a mysterious way
> his wonders to perform;
> he plants his footsteps in the sea,
> and rides upon the storm.
>
> Deep in unfathomable mines
> of never-failing skill
> he treasures up his bright designs,
> and works his sov'reign will.[2]

Terrified

The disciples are suddenly "terrified" (Matt. 14:26). It isn't only the ferocity of the storm that makes them afraid; it is the sight of Jesus walking through the storm "on the sea" at around 4 a.m. (v. 25).

It is "the fourth watch of the night" (between 3 and 6 a.m.; v. 25). This means that the disciples have been at sea for more than nine hours. Jesus has made them wait. He could have come to them at the very beginning of the storm, but He did not. For reasons known only to Him, He wanted them to experience the trial for a certain amount of time. It was a test. Trials always test our faith.

What was Jesus doing all this time? Praying! He had ascended a mountain near the shore "to pray" (v. 23).

Why should the Son of God need to pray? After all, He holds the universe in the palm of His hand. He dictates the course of history. Are not the forces of the universe, including the powers of darkness, subject to His will? Why, then, does He pray?

Before answering that question, it's worth noting that Jesus' praying on this occasion was not an anomaly. He prayed after His baptism, in the morning before heading to Galilee, after healing people, before choosing the twelve disciples, before feeding the five thousand, while healing a deaf and mute man, before feeding the four thousand, at Caesarea Philippi when He asked the disciples who people thought He was, at the transfiguration, at the return of the seventy-two, before giving the disciples the Lord's Prayer, before raising Lazarus from the dead, when He blessed little children and laid His hands on them, at the Last Supper, for Peter when Satan asked that he might sift him as wheat, in the upper room the night before His death, in Gethsemane, when nailed to the cross, in His dying breath, and before eating bread with His disciples in His resurrection body.[3] In short, it's probably not an exaggeration to suggest that Jesus was always praying. It formed an essential pattern of His daily life.

But to go back to the original question: Why? The answer lies in the reality of His incarnation. In the words of the Nicene Creed, Jesus is "God of God, . . . very God of very God, begotten, not made, being of one substance with the Father, by whom all things were made." But He is also human. He has a human body and a human soul. He has a human mind and a human will. In His earthly life, He experienced pain, hunger, and thirst. More profoundly, He experienced death, the separation of body and soul.

Jesus' prayers indicate that according to His humanity, He was utterly dependent on His heavenly Father's support and provision while on earth. He lived by faith in the tenderhearted encouragement of His Father. He was dependent on His Father for food, strength, knowledge, and insight. All that Jesus did was by the ministry of the Holy Spirit, in utter dependence on His Father. He did not pray simply to set an example for His disciples. He prayed because He could not survive without it. The One who walked on the Sea of

Galilee was at the same time wholly dependent on the sustaining power of the Holy Spirit.

Even the Winds and the Sea Obey Him

As we have already noted, this was not the first storm at sea that the disciples had witnessed. Earlier they had been in a boat, this time with Jesus, who was sound asleep. It is a testimony to the reality of His true humanity that the disciples had to wake Him up, saying, "Save us, Lord; we are perishing" (Matt. 8:25). He had been so utterly exhausted that not even a storm could wake Him! Chiding them for their "little faith," He rebuked the storm, and there was "a great calm" (v. 26). The disciples marveled, saying, "What sort of man is this, that even winds and sea obey him?" (v. 27).

Evidently, the memory of that miracle has now faded. The men are not expecting Jesus to repeat the miracle, and most certainly they are not expecting Jesus to walk on the Sea of Galilee straight into the storm. Instead, when they see the form of someone walking on the water but cannot make out who (or what) it is, they jump to the conclusion that "it is a ghost!" (Matt. 14:26).

The Jewish people had a love-hate relationship with the sea. Although technically they had access to the Mediterranean, for much of Israel's history the coastline was occupied by Israel's enemies. And Leviathan, the great, mythical, Ugaritic sea monster, loomed large in the nation's consciousness (cf. Job 3:8; 41:1; Pss. 74:14; 104:26; Isa. 27:1). This may in part explain the fact that the disciples are suddenly "terrified" (Matt. 14:26). Until, that is, they hear a familiar voice, saying: "Take heart; it is I. Do not be afraid" (v. 27). In the previous chapter, we pointed out the frequency with which the Bible employs the refrain "do not be afraid." Fear is conquered when Jesus is near.

Many twentieth-century New Testament scholars scoffed at this miraculous event, trying to explain it away by claiming that the boat was merely in shallow water, near bulrushes close to the shore. Antisupernaturalism, the consequence of the Enlightenment, drove them to these conclusions. To accommodate Scripture to "science" and a more modern understanding of the universe, theologically liberal scholars quietly removed miracles. But at what cost? Since the entrance and exit of Jesus into and out of this world involves the supernatural, opposition to the miraculous undoes the very essence of

Christianity. Without the miraculous, there is no Jesus. And without Jesus, there is no gospel.

The Greek is stubbornly unsympathetic to this accommodation to antisupernaturalism, using the word "on" (*epi*), not *in* (*se* or *entōs*), for Jesus' relation to the water (Matt. 14:25; cf. vv. 28–29). It is as if Peter is saying: "I was there. And Jesus was *on* the water. And so was I, for a minute or two."

Triumph and Failure

What happened next is so typical of Peter. It is what endears him to us. If, as we suggested earlier, Peter is the one telling this story to Matthew, Peter tells it without attempting to dilute his tragic lapse of faith.

Peter's initial response to hearing Jesus call out to the disciples was to ask Jesus to allow him to do the same. And Jesus did. Peter got out of the boat and walked toward Jesus. He was walking on water, defying the laws of gravity and density.

Was it bravado? That Jesus bid Peter come to Him suggests otherwise. None of Jesus' miracles lacks significance, and none is a mere display of showmanship. All of them are purposeful. And this one demonstrated that the winds and waves obey His voice.

Why not have all the disciples walk on the sea? The obvious answer is that only Peter suggested it. Perhaps the rest thought that Peter was crazy. And it was Peter's faith that needed to be tested if he was to fulfill the special role that Jesus had planned for him.

What is faith capable of? A great deal, according to Jesus. Upon seeing a ripe fig tree wither in seconds, Jesus told the disciples: "Truly, I say to you, if you have faith and do not doubt, you will not only do what has been done to the fig tree, but even if you say to this mountain, 'Be taken up and thrown into the sea,' it will happen. And whatever you ask in prayer, you will receive, if you have faith" (Matt. 21:21–22).

This is the same Peter who would later urge Christians to resist the devil, "*firm* in [their] faith" (1 Peter 5:9, emphasis added).

But Peter's faith failed him. When faith in Jesus becomes faith in faith, it always does. He looked away from his Savior and calculated the illogicality of it all. And viscosity took over. He was heavier than water, and the laws of the universe asserted themselves. His faith became "little faith" and quickly turned into doubt (Matt. 14:31).

This is often the tempter's ploy. In C.S. Lewis' *The Screwtape Letters*, an apprentice demon is being schooled in the art of casting doubt:

> But there is an even better way of exploiting the trough; I mean through the patient's own thoughts about it. As always, the first step is to keep knowledge out of his mind. Do not let him suspect the law of undulation. Let him assume that the first ardours of his conversion might have been expected to last, and ought to have lasted, forever, and that his present dryness is an equally permanent condition. Having once got this misconception well fixed in his head, you may then proceed in various ways. It all depends on whether your man is of the desponding type who can be tempted to despair, or of the wishful-thinking type who can be assured that all is well. The former type is getting rare among the humans. If your patient should happen to belong to it, everything is easy. You have only got to keep him out of the way of experienced Christians (an easy task nowadays), to direct his attention to the appropriate passages in scripture, and then to set him to work on the desperate design of recovering his old feelings by sheer will-power, and the game is ours. If he is of the more hopeful type, your job is to make him acquiesce in the present low temperature of his spirit and gradually become content with it, persuading himself that it is not so low after all. In a week or two you will be making him doubt whether the first days of his Christianity were not, perhaps, a little excessive. Talk to him about "moderation in all things." If you can once get him to the point of thinking that "religion is all very well up to a point," you can feel quite happy about his soul. A moderated religion is as good for us as no religion at all—and more amusing.[4]

Worship

After Jesus and Peter are safely inside the boat, the wind ceases, and the disciples are amazed. Once again, they are overcome by the knowledge that they are in the presence of One who is holy and powerful. They do the only thing they can do. They *worship* Him (Matt. 14:33).

There is nothing fouler to the Jewish mindset than idolatry. It bedeviled the narrative of the Israelites' entire history. That there is only one God who deserves to be worshiped was a canon emblazoned on their hearts. It was enshrined in the Ten Commandments. And yet these Jewish Christians are worshiping Jesus. And Jesus does not reprimand them. He gladly accepts their worship.

The disciples recognized again that this man from Nazareth, the son of Mary and Joseph, was also God. For everything else about which the disciples are confused, there is no doubt about the divinity of Jesus in the Gospels on the part of the disciples. The early disciples accepted as fact that Jesus is *God*. This truth about Jesus is as simple as it is astonishing and beautiful all at the same time. More importantly, without this fact, there is no Christianity. In the boat on the Sea of Galilee that morning was God Himself.

4

To Whom
Shall We Go?

In 1519, Hernán Cortés, at the time in Cuba, led an expedition to explore what we know as Mexico, where he would eventually overthrow the vast and powerful Aztec Empire. Upon arrival, for complicated reasons involving Cuba, Spain, and Emperor Charles V, Cortés scuttled his ships, forcing his men to act as infantry. There was no going back.[1]

But with Jesus, it is different. If you want to stop being a disciple and go back to what you once were, He might not stop you!

We learn this from John, when he says, "After this many of his disciples turned back and no longer walked with him" (John 6:66). Crowds had gathered to hear Jesus preach and witness His miracles. He fed them with some loaves and fish from a boy's lunchbox, identified by Peter's brother Andrew (vv. 8–9). Those were splendid times on the mountain. Now Jesus is back in Capernaum, teaching in the synagogue (v. 59). But this time, there are no giveaways to receive or miracles to witness, just lots of teaching and preaching. So many decide to leave and go home—and not just to go back to work. John is suggesting that their return was something more. The Apostle focuses on the fact that they "no longer walked with [Jesus]" (v. 66). Even more alarmingly, Jesus warns that one of the twelve disciples is a "devil" (v. 70).

No one saw that coming. John identifies the disciple in question, after the fact, as Judas Iscariot (v. 71). But the disciples, including Peter, must have been asking themselves, "Is it me?"

Apostasy and betrayal are all too real in the kingdom of God. Jesus wants us to know about this so that we can be watchful. Peter must have thought about it often. He wrote in his first epistle: "Be sober-minded; be watchful. Your adversary the devil prowls around like a roaring lion, seeking someone to devour" (1 Peter 5:8).

The devil is trying to get you to walk away from Jesus.

You must fight the devil.

Hard Sayings

What are some of the reasons that might stop us from walking with Jesus? There are many, but in John 6:60–71, we find that one cause of apathy and indifference is the hard things that Jesus says. And John specifically relates that it was Jesus' "disciples" who complain, "This is a hard saying; who can listen to it?" (v. 60). This is a reference not to the twelve disciples or Apostles but to disciples generally.

What had Jesus said that caused His disciples to grumble and Jesus to respond, "Do you take offense at this?" (v. 61). It had to do with something Jesus said about eating His flesh and drinking His blood (v. 53).

There has been and continues to be much discussion about whether John is giving us his version of the Last Supper, where similar words are used. It is curious that the second half of John's gospel concentrates entirely on the last week of Jesus' earthly life, four of the chapters providing a detailed account of what Jesus said and did in the upper room on the eve of His crucifixion, but that there is no mention of the Last Supper. Some, therefore, propose that John has already told us about the supper liturgy in John 6.

The explanation is less than convincing. Because Jesus would repeat similar but not identical language at the inauguration of the Lord's Supper, the language of eating His flesh and drinking His blood has appealed to those who advocate a transubstantiation view,[2] as in the Roman Catholic Mass. We need, then, to ask what Jesus meant by eating His flesh and drinking His blood. If we take what He says in John 6:40 and 6:53 together, we seem to arrive at an answer.

> "For this is the will of my Father, that everyone who looks on the Son and believes in him should have eternal life, and I will raise him up on the last day." (v. 40)

"Truly, truly, I say to you, unless you eat the flesh of the Son of Man and drink his blood, you have no life in you." (v. 53)

Eating the flesh of Christ and *drinking the blood of Christ* are the same as *looking to the Son* and *believing in Him*. The eating and drinking are meant to be understood as spiritual equivalents for having and exercising faith in Christ.

Still, the saying is hard, both for Jesus' disciples and for us.

Books have been written on the hard sayings of Jesus.[3] These hard sayings include the following:

- "If anyone comes to me and does not hate his own father and mother and wife and children and brothers and sisters, yes, and even his own life, he cannot be my disciple." (Luke 14:26)
- "For I tell you, unless your righteousness exceeds that of the scribes and Pharisees, you will never enter the kingdom of heaven." (Matt. 5:20)
- "You therefore must be perfect, as your heavenly Father is perfect." (Matt. 5:48)
- "And do not fear those who kill the body but cannot kill the soul. Rather fear him who can destroy both soul and body in hell." (Matt. 10:28)
- "Leave the dead to bury their own dead." (Matt. 8:22)
- "And let the one who has no sword sell his cloak and buy one." (Luke 22:36)

To be sure, there are more!

Having mentioned these sayings here, I suspect that your minds will begin to wonder what they mean. But we must not get distracted. The point here is simply that Jesus often spoke in a way that was difficult. He spoke in parables, and when His disciples asked why He did this, His response was in effect "to keep unbelievers from understanding what I say!" (cf. Matt. 13:10–15).

Jesus did not feel the need to dumb everything down. Sometimes, as they say, He placed the cookies on the top shelf. If you can't be bothered to do some hard study to understand what Jesus wants you to know, it may be a sign that you are walking *away* from Him.

Offensive Sayings

Some of the things that Jesus said were not only difficult to grasp but difficult to *accept*. The disciples were "grumbling," and Jesus heard them (John 6:61). Things that Jesus had said caused them to take *offense*.

We live in a culture in which taking offense has become the norm. Some have made "virtue signaling" a fine (or coarse) art. People are easily offended by anyone who doesn't think as they do. They have become professional offense takers, hardwired to be triggered by any countercultural statement.

The church, sadly, is not immune to this culture. It often begins with someone's saying, "I could never believe in a God who would do *x* or forbid *y*." The measure of what is offensive is the *person's* set of values (or lack thereof) rather than God's revealed Word. In a postmodern culture, we provide our own values and are offended when they are questioned or ignored.

Many things in Scripture offend today's culture. Here are just a few of them:

- Binary sex
- Marriage *only* between one man and one woman
- Sex *only* within marriage
- The roles of men and women within marriage
- Women and preaching
- Women and office in the church
- The doctrine of hell and eternal, conscious suffering

Evidently, the disciples did not like the direction that Jesus was going in saying that they must eat His flesh and drink His blood. Did they imagine some form of ritualistic cannibalism? But instead of asking Him to explain further, they started grumbling. Maybe Peter remembered this exchange with Jesus when he urged his readers to "show hospitality to one another without grumbling" (1 Peter 4:9). Likewise, recalling the exodus, Paul, in a context that leads to some hard teaching on the Lord's Supper, which the Corinthians were terribly abusing, wrote, "We must not put Christ to the test, as some of them did and were destroyed by serpents, nor grumble, as some of them did and were destroyed by the Destroyer" (1 Cor. 10:9–10). Grumbling is a sure sign that you are heading *away* from Jesus.

Jesus' way of dealing with the offense taken by the disciples is to push the accelerator, saying something like, "If you're offended by what I just said, what will you think when I ascend, a process that begins by My first being nailed to a cross and crucified?" (cf. John 6:62). The problem that seems to be present in the disciples' minds is that they are not in charge of the narrative. Faith calls us to believe in everything Jesus said, including the hard and *seemingly* offensive things.

Humbling Things

The root problem within the inner circle of disciples was pride. They needed to see that they required the help of the Holy Spirit to understand the spiritual things that Jesus was saying. "It is the Spirit who gives life; the flesh is no help at all" (John 6:63).

Among His disciples were those who did *not* believe. Most obviously, a betrayer was present (vv. 64–65). They needed to be humbled. And nothing is more humbling than knowing that no one can come to Jesus in faith "unless it is granted him by the Father" (v. 65). The doctrine of election is the greatest humbler of all. That statement alone cuts the legs from underneath you. The high doctrines of election and prevenient grace (grace working in us before we are able to respond) are truths designed to humble our proud, peacock-feathered hearts. Sin is crouching at the door, and the disciples must reject it before it overpowers them (cf. Gen. 4:7).

Then comes the sting. Jesus asks the disciples, "Do you want to go away as well?" (John 6:67).

It must have shocked them when He asked this question.

Enter Peter the Fearless! In words that must have sounded like the voice of an archangel, Peter responds: "Lord, to whom shall we go? You have the words of eternal life, and we have believed, and have come to know, that you are the Holy One of God" (vv. 68–69).

Magnificent! Who but Peter would come out with such a reply?

"The Holy One of God." Jesus is the One whom the Father has set apart as Messiah. There is *no one else* to whom Peter and the disciples can turn. And Peter will echo the sentiment again, after Pentecost, fearlessly preaching in Jerusalem before a hostile crowd, "And there is salvation in no one else, for there is no other name under heaven given among men by which we must be saved" (Acts 4:12).

There is no Savior to rescue us from our sin other than Jesus. Why should you think of walking away from Him and abandon all hope of salvation?

I heard the voice of Jesus say,
"Come unto me and rest;
lay down, O weary one, lay down
your head upon my breast."
I came to Jesus as I was,
weary and worn and sad;
I found in him a resting place,
and he has made me glad.

I heard the voice of Jesus say,
"Behold, I freely give
the living water; thirsty one,
stoop down and drink, and live."
I came to Jesus, and I drank
of that life-giving stream;
my thirst was quenched, my soul revived,
and now I live in him.

I heard the voice of Jesus say,
"I am this dark world's Light;
look unto me, your morn shall rise,
and all your day be bright."
I looked to Jesus and I found
in him my Star, my Sun;
and in that light of life I'll walk,
till trav'ling days are done.[4]

5

Jesus Has
Only One Plan

Jesus has only one plan. And it's called "church." He revealed the plan to Peter at Caesarea Philippi, some twenty-five miles north of the Sea of Galilee in the foothills of Mount Hermon.

It was Peter that Jesus singled out, saying to him, "And I tell you, you are Peter, and on this rock I will build my church, and the gates of hell shall not prevail against it" (Matt. 16:18). Few can hear a statement like this and not be filled with pride. To be referred to as "number one" can swell your head in a heartbeat. I doubt that for the rest of his life, Peter ever went to sleep at night without recalling this moment in Caesarea Philippi.

Peter, of course, didn't handle it without a misstep. But we'll get to that later. For now, we focus on Jesus' plan to build His church.

Like Julius Caesar's crossing of the river Rubicon with his army, this moment at Caesarea Philippi was a turning point in Jesus' ministry. Named in honor of himself and Emperor Augustus by Philip the Tetrarch, the city had been known as Paneas, associating the city with Pan, the Greek god of desolate places and fortune.[1] It is difficult to be certain, but we are about a year and a half, possibly two years, into Jesus' ministry. Up until this point, Jesus has kept His identity and mission relatively secret. Scholars refer to this initial period as the *messianic secret*. But all that is about to change.

Even though "Messiah" ("Christ" [*Christos* in the Greek New Testament]) is the most frequently used title for Jesus by New Testament writers as they wrote decades later, it was not a title that Jesus used with any frequency.

Passages such as Mark 3:12; 5:43; 8:30; Luke 8:56; 9:21 show that Jesus forcefully commanded His disciples to keep His identity secret on occasion. That may appear very strange to us. Had He not come into the world to be the Messiah? Yes, but messianic expectations in first-century Judea were intense and varied.

For example, there was a significant expectation on the part of some (the Sicarii) that the Messiah would raise up an army to conquer and defeat the Roman occupation of Israel and return it to the glorious days of King David. The Sicarii carried weapons and were also known as Zealots. Among Jesus' twelve disciples was Simon the Zealot (Luke 6:15), and some have suggested that he may, at some point, have been sympathetic to the Sicarii agenda of a violent uprising against Rome.

Another expectation was that the Messiah would restore Israel's fortunes immediately, without the need for a crucifixion or a prolonged second coming. Even the Apostles were confused about this after Jesus' resurrection, when they asked Him, "Lord, will you at this time restore the kingdom to Israel?" (Acts 1:6). Evidently, the disciples had not grasped all that Jesus had taught them.

Jesus had a perfect plan. He had to die at the appointed time, in the appointed manner, for the appointed reason. His death had to be in accord with the prophetic writings of Isaiah, as a Suffering Servant. On some occasions (e.g., John 4:26), He disclosed His identity to those closest to Him, knowing that His "secret" was safe with them. But here, at Caesarea Philippi, the secret is out. Peter discloses it in a magnificent testimony to His identity as "the Christ, the Son of the living God" (Matt. 16:16).

Who Is Jesus?

"Who do people say that the Son of Man is?" (Matt. 16:13). This is the question that Jesus puts to His disciples. And there were many answers. Some thought He was John the Baptist returned from the dead (his death is recorded in 14:1–12). Jesus and His cousin John the Baptist were almost the same age (John was six months older), and they had been seen together, so they could hardly be the same person. Perhaps some thought that the "spirit" of John had returned to occupy his cousin Jesus.

Others thought that He might be Elijah. Since Elijah had been taken into heaven alive (2 Kings 2:11), an expectation of his return developed, and to this day, Orthodox Jews keep an empty chair for Elijah at the celebration of Seder, or Passover.

Still others answered the question by recounting that some people thought Jesus was Jeremiah or one of the other prophets.

What emerges from these answers is significant. Though these answers were incorrect, there was no doubt that people had very definite opinions about who Jesus was. He had made a mark, and people were forced to reckon with His identity. His fame was widespread.

Who is Jesus of Nazareth? The question remains as valid—and essential— now as it was then. Entertaining a postmodern view of history that doubts His very existence is simply to bury one's head in the sand. There is more evidence for Jesus' existence than for any other person in all history. But again, who is He? It remains a fundamental question. And the answer changes everything. In today's sensitive culture, some people balk at dividing history into *BC* and *AD*, "before Christ" and "in the year of our Lord," so they employ the more neutral *BCE*, "before the common era," and *CE*, "common [or current] era." But it still raises the question why there is a *before* and an *after*. And the answer is that Jesus Christ changed the very course of history. Indeed, *BCE* and *CE* are nothing more than weak attempts to ignore Jesus without recognizing that the dividing line is Jesus.

In the 2022 Ligonier State of Theology survey, 43 percent of evangelicals rejected the deity of Christ.[2] For some, Jesus is someone who inspires them to live better. For others, He is one of many faith leaders, along with Muhammad and Vishnu. For others, He is a name on a T-shirt. Even scholars invent narratives about His identity. As just one example, Barbara Thiering, in her book *Jesus & the Riddle of the Dead Sea Scrolls*,[3] tells a fantastical tale that Jesus recovered in the tomb, married twice, and fathered three children. When basic rules about the nature of history are abandoned, there is no limit to invention.

Perhaps the best place to start in answering the question about Jesus' identity is to ask how Jesus Himself would have answered the question. Of course, we cannot fully answer that question without a conviction that the Scriptures, the source for our answer, are the inerrant Word of God. Apart from this conviction, we cannot fully answer the question with any degree of certainty.

Confining ourselves to the episode at Caesarea Philippi, Jesus answers the question in the question He put to the disciples: "Who do people say that the Son of Man is?" (Matt. 16:13). Jesus self-identified as "the Son of Man." It is Jesus' most frequent self-designation.

In the eighteenth and nineteenth centuries, it was common for conservative commentaries to suggest that the expression "Son of God" referred to Christ's deity and "Son of Man" to His humanity. But this was an error. The title "Son of Man" comes from one of Daniel's night visions of the heavenly courtroom:

> And behold, with the clouds of heaven
> there came one like a son of man,
> and he came to the Ancient of Days
> and was presented before him. (Dan. 7:13)

In Daniel's vision, the Ancient of Days is being enthroned, in preparation for the judgment. And to the Ancient of Days is sent "one like a son of man" who is given authority to carry out the judgment.

This title is not a description of Jesus' humanity. It is instead a proclamation that He has authority to judge the world. By His word, humanity will rise or fall. It is a divine title, and Jesus deliberately chose it as a description of who He is. Jesus comes into the world to judge the world, but then He returns with the clouds of heaven into the presence of the Ancient of Days.

Two examples of Jesus' use of the title "Son of Man" clearly show its divine significance. First, earlier in Matthew, when the Pharisees complained that Jesus' disciples picked some grain on the Sabbath, Jesus responded that "something greater than the temple is here. . . . For the Son of Man is lord of the Sabbath" (Matt. 12:6, 8). Second, when Jesus healed a paralytic in Capernaum, He said to the paralytic, "Son, your sins are forgiven" (Mark 2:5). Only God can forgive sins. Yet Jesus said without any equivocation that "the Son of Man has authority on earth to forgive sins" (v. 10). The scribes present for this event knew that that power belonged solely to God, which is why they were offended by what Jesus did, accusing Him of blasphemy (vv. 6–7). Either Jesus was a blasphemer or He was God. His claim is the latter.

Christ, the Son of the Living God

Peter's answer to Jesus' question about His identity came straight out of heaven. Flesh and blood had not revealed it to him, Jesus declared, but "[Jesus'] Father who is in heaven" (Matt. 16:17).

Two further titles are now employed affirming Jesus' true identity: "You are the Christ, the Son of the living God" (v. 16). Like "Son of Man," the term "Christ" is not a name but a title. We sometimes forget that fact when we call Him Jesus Christ. The title is derived from the Greek *Christos*, meaning "anointed one." Prophets, priests, and kings in the Old Testament were given the title "anointed one" because they had been anointed and set apart for special tasks. These figures were anticipations, foreshadowing *the* Anointed One who was to come. Strikingly, the pagan Persian king Cyrus was even given this title because of his decree to allow the exiles to return to Jerusalem (Isa. 45:1).

Jesus is the "Son of God" in two senses. First, He is the incarnate Jesus, possessing a body of flesh and blood, with a human mind, will, and self-awareness. According to His humanity, He has not always existed, and He can be present in only one location at any one point of time. And He is capable of being killed—look no further than Calvary. But there is also the *eternal* Son of God, the second person of the Trinity, who has always existed and who is omniscient, omnipresent, and omnipotent. When Jesus uses this name for Himself, He means it in the latter sense. Even the unbelieving Jews knew what Jesus intended when using this name. In His final hours, Jesus was brought to Pilate for judgment, but Pilate could find no wrong in Him. Yet the Jews pleaded, "We have a law, and according to that law he ought to die because he has made himself the Son of God" (John 19:7). Jesus was crucified because of His claim to be the "Son of God," a claim that the Jews found profane.

So the question is, Are we willing to believe Jesus' claim to be God?

Believing this claim has consequences. If Jesus is God, you must believe *everything* He said. And if Jesus is God, you must *worship* Him.

I Will Build My Church

We discussed in chapter 1 that in Peter's first encounter with Jesus, Peter's name became its Aramaic version—"Cephas" (John 1:42). Because *Cephas* means "rock" in Aramaic, Peter was being given anticipation of what occurs here at Caesarea Philippi. Peter's name (Greek, *petros*) is almost a homophone for the Greek word for "rock" (*petra*). He will play a most significant part in the establishment of the New Testament church.

As we noted earlier, during the Reformation and post-Reformation periods, Roman Catholics and Protestants disagreed on what Jesus meant when He told Peter, "On this rock I will build my church" (Matt. 16:18). Roman Catholics wanted to raise Peter's importance and claim him as the first pope. Protestants pushed back, suggesting that the "rock" was a reference to Peter's *confession of Jesus' true identity* rather than a reference to Peter himself. Both appear to be wrong. Peter may not be the first pope, but Jesus is going to use Peter to advance His kingdom and build His church.

Several matters deserve some comment.

First is the use of the word "church" (Greek, *ekklēsia*). This is the first time in Matthew's gospel that the word is used. All we hear from Jesus up to this point is "kingdom." Where did "church" come from? The fact that no one asked Him what the word meant suggests very strongly that they understood what Jesus was saying.

The Greek word *ekklēsia* is itself derived from the Hebrew and literally means the "called-out assembly" or "congregation." Stephen, shortly before his death, in a lengthy sermon covering the history of the Old Testament as a preparation for the coming of Christ, referred to the people of God in the wilderness years as "the congregation in the wilderness" (Acts 7:38). The word "congregation" is *ekklēsia*. Some (Presbyterians, for example) insist that it should read "church in the wilderness," as in the King James Version, to make the point that "church" has been God's plan from the very beginning.

Jesus has only one plan, and it is called "church." This means that no Christian can be indifferent to Christ's church. Church is not an option. It is not a luxury. It is central to the purposes of God.

Second, Jesus builds His church in enemy-occupied territory, right next to "the gates of hell" (Matt. 16:18). The church is not in Eden but in the wilderness of this world, where enemies abound and Satan is near. Peter will know all too well that Satan lurks around every corner, and in a moment, Satan will overpower to the extent that Jesus refers to Peter as "Satan" (v. 23).

Third, the promise that Jesus gives to Peter is that the gates of hell will *not* prevail. "The reason the Son of God appeared was to destroy the works of the devil" (1 John 3:8). That promise, however, does not find fulfillment without resistance to Satan on our part. Peter wrote about it. After warning his readers that Satan prowls like a roaring lion, Peter exhorted them, "Resist him, firm in your faith" (1 Peter 5:9).

How is Jesus going to accomplish this task of building His church? More to the point, how in the world is *Peter* going to take on this task? Only God can bring sinners out of their innate darkness and into the light. Only the Holy Spirit can give a new heart. And Jesus is going to do it through using someone such as Peter. Yes! Because Jesus gives to Peter "the keys of the kingdom of heaven" that can "bind" and "loose" (Matt. 16:19). Again, there have been disagreements about the meaning of what Jesus is saying, and some have seen this as a reference to church discipline. But I rather think that a more obvious meaning is intended. Jesus is giving the key that unlocks the gate of heaven for sinners who cannot unlock it for themselves.

And what is that key? *The gospel.* It is "the power of God for salvation to everyone who believes" (Rom. 1:16). It is as though Jesus is saying to Peter: "The key is in your pocket. *Use it!*"

That is a great deal to take in, and Peter's head must have been reeling. Peter, as well as the other disciples, must ponder it and keep it secret for now (Matt. 16:20).

6

Getting It All Wrong

After Caesarea Philippi, Peter must have done a lot of thinking. He must have wondered about this new role that Jesus had spoken about. He, and only he, had been singled out. Thinking like this can swell the head. And it appears that Peter's head was a size or two larger than it had been.

Matthew doesn't tell us specifically when this incident took place, but it follows the time at Caesarea Philippi, given that Matthew writes "from that time" to introduce what follows as happening later (Matt. 16:21). Perhaps several weeks had passed.

Jesus' demeanor was often serious. He was "a man of sorrows" (Isa. 53:3). But now, He seems more somber than usual. He has a deeply troubling message to give to the disciples, one that they should have seen coming. But they did not. "From that time Jesus began to show his disciples that he must go to Jerusalem and suffer many things from the elders and chief priests and scribes, and be killed, and on the third day be raised" (Matt. 16:21).

From this point forward, the road leads inexorably toward Jerusalem. And there, in the beloved city, Jesus would be crucified.

Surely not!

To His disciples, such a notion was both unthinkable and deeply disturbing. Surely Jesus had come to redeem His people. The narrative they believed was a glorious one of victory and deliverance. This story cannot end with Jesus hanging on a cross! Where is the victory in that? Such a thing would only empower Rome even further! And though it was obvious that many Jews, especially the ones who hung around the temple in Jerusalem, were hostile to

Jesus, if He were to tone down His message a little, He might convince them that He is the promised Messiah after all. Peter must deliver Jesus from these dark thoughts and get Him to a better place.

Never, Lord!

Peter's response to all this talk about suffering and death was to rebuke Jesus: "Far be it from you, Lord! This shall never happen to you" (Matt. 16:22).

He calls Jesus "Lord" and tells Him that He is mistaken about His future.

There are two words that cannot be uttered together: "Never, Lord!"

These words, however misguided, came from Peter's love for Jesus. The thought that Jesus would be crucified broke his heart. He would do anything to prevent it.

What exactly had Jesus said? He had spoken of suffering, death, and resurrection. It was His destiny—He *must* go to Jerusalem. It was a plan ordered in the councils of eternity. It was the only way for salvation to be accomplished.

Some posit that if God is sovereign, He can simply will that sinners be saved. By an act of divine fiat, God can simply will whatever He pleases. But the Reformed tradition has thought otherwise. The Westminster Confession of Faith, for example, in its chapter on the work of Christ as the Mediator, states the following:

> The Lord Jesus, by his perfect obedience, and sacrifice of himself, which he, through the eternal Spirit, once offered up unto God, hath *fully satisfied the justice of his Father*; and purchased, not only reconciliation, but an everlasting inheritance in the kingdom of heaven, for all those whom the Father has given unto him.[1]

A similar statement occurs in the Heidelberg Catechism, which states that "the claims of [His] justice" must be satisfied.[2]

There are many ways to view what occurred at Calvary, and the Bible employs a variety of ideas. For example, Jesus was a substitute. He provided a propitiation for our sins. He was the Lamb of God. He was a sacrifice. The cross was the means of our justification. But these confessional statements place one aspect of the cross at the forefront: Jesus satisfied divine justice.

Satisfaction

The principal effect of the death of Christ is the satisfaction of divine justice. An important passage of Scripture that underlines this idea is Romans 3:21–26. The righteousness of God demands that the salvation of sinners be accomplished in a manner that reveals God to "be just and the justifier of the one who has faith in Jesus" (v. 26). The holiness of God cannot be sacrificed to procure forgiveness. Were God simply to declare forgiveness without the due process of justice, His very being would be in question.

How can satisfaction of divine justice be accomplished? One of two ways. Either the sinner receives the consequence of his sin or a substitute pays the price in his stead. And Jesus is telling Peter and the disciples, "I intend to stand in your place and suffer the wrath of God that your sins deserve."

Satisfaction and *substitution* are two of the principal words that get to the heart of the redemptive work of Christ. Together, they encapsulate what the cross is all about. There is no divine necessity for God to save anyone. But having determined to save, God has no way to accomplish it other than the substitutionary death of Jesus, satisfying the demands of divine justice.

For Peter, this was too much. So he voiced his objection. Such a thing could never happen to his beloved Jesus. And Jesus responded quickly and pointedly: "You are not setting your mind on the things of God, but on the things of man" (Matt. 16:23). Peter was thinking in a human way. He wasn't thinking from the point of view of God. His thinking was earthbound and skewed. Whatever his motivation for blurting out this objection, he had entirely missed the divine perspective. He had not sufficiently considered the weightiness of sin and the cost of its forgiveness.

And behind Peter's exclamation lay the voice of the evil one.

From one point of view, it is quite surprising that Jesus should address Peter with the words "Get behind me, Satan!" (v. 23). He had never before spoken to any of His disciples in this way, not even to Judas Iscariot. Why the sudden outburst? Perhaps because Peter's words reminded Jesus of a similar suggestion offered to Him in the wilderness when Satan had urged Him to achieve His crown without the sufferings of Calvary:

> Again, the devil took him to a very high mountain and showed him all the
> kingdoms of the world and their glory. And he said to him, "All these I will

give you, if you will fall down and worship me." Then Jesus said to him, "Be gone, Satan! For it is written,

> "'You shall worship the Lord your God
> and him only shall you serve.'" (Matt. 4:8–10)

Peter's words too closely echoed what Satan had suggested to Jesus. What Satan had offered Jesus was a *real* temptation. We should not lessen the allurement. And that offer resounded unsettlingly in the words of Peter. Such an offer had to be rebuffed, quickly and decisively, and its true source identified, accurately and immediately. Peter, at this moment, was a tool of Satan. The evil one had entered Peter's thinking. This was not an occasion to spare Peter's feelings. Peter was on the wrong side, and he needed to know it.

It must have been a memory that Peter recalled many times in the years that followed, a memory that made him warn fellow Christians that Satan prowls about us like a roaring lion, seeking whom he may devour. We must resist him, just as Jesus did (1 Peter 5:8–9).

Cross-Bearing and Self-Denial

Having spoken of His own suffering on behalf of His disciples, a suffering that achieves their salvation, Jesus turns to address Peter and his fellow disciples. They, too, are called to a life of suffering.

> Go, labor on: spend and be spent,
> your joy to do the Father's will;
> it is the way the Master went;
> should not the servant tread it still?[3]

What does it mean to be a disciple of Jesus? Jesus answered this question, telling Peter and the rest of the disciples: "If anyone would come after me, let him deny himself and take up his cross and follow me. For whoever would save his life will lose it, but whoever loses his life for my sake will find it. For what will it profit a man if he gains the whole world and forfeits his soul? Or what shall a man give in return for his soul?" (Matt. 16:24–26).

Jesus does not desire half-hearted discipleship. Following Jesus must be all or nothing. He wants us to be all in. Not 50 percent but 100 percent. He desires all there is of us. Body and soul. Heart and mind. Will and affections.

Peter's rebuke came from his love for Jesus. But it likely also came from fear. If Jesus was to suffer, His disciples would too. Jesus had said as much on an earlier occasion: "A disciple is not above his teacher, nor a servant above his master. It is enough for the disciple to be like his teacher, and the servant like his master. If they have called the master of the house Beelzebul, how much more will they malign those of his household" (Matt. 10:24–25). And Peter had no doubt witnessed crucifixions, the standard method of execution in the Roman Empire. It is understandable that he would be terrified at the prospect. Peter did not yet know that "taking up a cross" was going to be all too literal for both Jesus and His disciples.

If Peter's grasp of the way of salvation was lacking at first, it blossomed later:

> For to this you have been called, because Christ also suffered for you, leaving you an example, so that you might follow in his steps. He committed no sin, neither was deceit found in his mouth. When he was reviled, he did not revile in return; when he suffered, he did not threaten, but continued entrusting himself to him who judges justly. He himself bore our sins in his body on the tree, that we might die to sin and live to righteousness. By his wounds you have been healed. For you were straying like sheep, but have now returned to the Shepherd and Overseer of your souls. (1 Peter 2:21–25)

Jesus told Peter that to save his life, a disciple of Christ must be willing to lose it (Matt. 16:25). We may gain "the whole world" but forfeit our souls (v. 26).

John Calvin committed almost all of book 3 of his *Institutes of the Christian Religion* to the idea of discipleship. Principally, discipleship consists in self-denial, cross-bearing, and meditation on the future life. This section of the *Institutes* has been printed separately, and a recent translation puts the matter of obedience clearly:

> If, then, we want to be disciples of Christ, we should make it our aim to soak our minds in the sort of sensitivity and obedience to God that can tame and

subdue every natural impulse contrary to His command. So it will be that no matter what kind of cross is placed upon us, we will steadily maintain endurance even through the narrowest straits of the soul. Indeed, adverse circumstances will keep their bitterness, and we will feel their bite. When afflicted by illness, we will groan and toss and long for health. When pursued by poverty, we will feel the stings of sadness and anxiety. We will bear the weight of sorrow at dishonor, and injustice. When loved ones die, we will naturally weep. But this will always be our conclusion: Nevertheless, the Lord has willed it. Therefore, let us follow His will. Indeed, this thought must intervene in the midst of sorrow's very stings, in the midst of our groans and tears, in order to incline our hearts to endure those things with which they're inflicted.[4]

Days before the Nazis executed him, Dietrich Bonhoeffer wrote in his journal:

The cross is laid on every Christian. The first Christ-suffering which every man must experience is the call to abandon the attachments of this world. It is that dying of the old man which is the result of his encounter with Christ. As we embark upon discipleship we surrender ourselves to Christ in union with His death—we give over our lives to death. Thus it begins; the cross is not the terrible end to an otherwise God-fearing and happy life, but it meets us at the beginning of our communion with Christ.

When Christ calls a man, He bids him come and die. It may be a death like that of the first disciples who had to leave home and work to follow Him, or it may be a death like Luther's, who had to leave the monastery and go out into the world. But it is the same death every time—death in Jesus Christ, the death of the old man at his call.[5]

These are sobering words that every Christian must take to heart.

7

The Transfiguration

There had never been anything like the transfiguration. It was a spectacular and unique moment in the earthly life of Jesus. Peter, along with the two brothers James and John, was singled out to witness it. Having spoken of His impending crucifixion, Jesus cast aside all doubt about His identity and revealed His glory. Something from the other side passed into this world, and for a moment, Jesus' appearance was altered. Even His clothing was affected; it now "became dazzling white" (Luke 9:29).

A week has passed.[1] Peter and the other disciples must have been pondering, with some alarm, the dark words that Jesus had uttered about His impending crucifixion. And perhaps Peter, especially, was nursing his wounds after having been so sharply rebuked by his Master. But something was about to happen that would cheer him up. He was about to taste something of the glory.

Suddenly, Jesus called on Peter, James, and John, and they proceeded to ascend a mountain. The Scriptures do not record which mountain it was, but Origen, in the third century, identified it as Mount Tabor.[2] In the twentieth century, a Franciscan Church of the Transfiguration was built on that site.

The reason given for this ascent was that Jesus needed to pray (Luke 9:28). We have commented on this need before as demonstrating the humanity of Jesus. According to His divinity, He had no need for prayer, but according to His human nature, He was weak and frail, just as we are (Heb. 4:15). In addition, He needed the help and support of His Father to perform the task that was set before Him. He needed reassurance that His Father would not abandon Him. He needed courage to complete the task. Given His words in Gethsemane, "Father, if you are willing, remove this cup from me" (Luke

22:42), that courage almost abandoned Him. Every day, Jesus was upheld by the Holy Spirit. And now, more than ever, Jesus needed the Spirit's fullness.

As He prayed, "the appearance of his face was altered, and his clothing became dazzling white" (Luke 9:29). Matthew puts it this way: "And he was transfigured before them, and his face shone like the sun, and his clothes became white as light" (Matt. 17:2). And Mark records it similarly: "And he was transfigured before them, and his clothes became radiant, intensely white, as no one on earth could bleach them" (Mark 9:2–3). The word "transfigured" in Greek is *metamorphōthēi*. Jesus experienced a metamorphosis.

We need to ensure that we do not misunderstand what happened. This experience was not a *deification*. Jesus' human nature was not now becoming a mixture of His divine and human natures. In the fifth century, Eutyches of Constantinople (c. 380–456) argued that the divine and human natures of Jesus are related as a mixture, a *third* nature. This view was roundly condemned as a heresy at the Council of Chalcedon in AD 451. Whatever the explanation for the alteration of His appearance and the radiance of His clothing, it must be understood in a way that maintains the full integrity of His human nature. Jesus was displaying what His human nature will look like in heaven. He had taken on a human nature in a world of sin. In Paul's words, without denying the absolute perfection (sinlessness) of Jesus, God sent His own Son "in the likeness of sinful flesh" (Rom. 8:3). In a world of sin, His flesh appeared weary and strained. But on the other side, there is glory. It remains human, but it is humanity *glorified*. And Jesus is being given a foretaste of it. As, of course, are Peter, James, and John.

But there was something even more strange. Moses and Elijah were there too. And they were talking with Jesus. They had come, as it were, through a veil that separates this world from heaven. Heaven is, after all, just a veil's width away. When we die, our souls pass into it. It is a veil that angels have passed through to minister to God's people.

Moses and Elijah are significant representatives of the Old Testament. They both played an important role in the advancement of the kingdom of God. They are there to speak to Jesus, to encourage Him.

Exodus

Moses and Elijah spoke to Jesus about His "departure" (Luke 9:31). In Greek, it is *exodos*. Moses knew a great deal about what an *exodus* might mean! He had victoriously delivered God's people from Egypt into the wilderness. He had led them through the watery ordeal of the sea that drowned His enemies. And now, in Jesus' departure from this world, He, too, will deliver His people. Had He not spoken of a watery ordeal, a *baptism*, that awaited Him? "I have a baptism to be baptized with, and how great is my distress until it is accomplished!" (12:50).

In the first place, it is important that we understand that the transfiguration was for Jesus' benefit. How did He know who He was? That is a question that might appear strange. After all, was He not God? And as God, He knew everything, including His own identity. But that is to confuse the two natures. In His human nature, He had to learn to speak. Luke tells us about this on two separate occasions: first when He was presented as a small child in the temple, "the child grew and became strong, filled with wisdom" (2:40), and later when He was twelve, "Jesus increased in wisdom and in stature" (v. 52).

In the fourth and fifth centuries, Apollinaris of Laodicea, a bishop of Syria (d. AD 382), was a stout defender of the deity of Christ, in opposition to Arius, who had coined the saying "There was a time when the Son was not." But in opposing Arianism, Apollinaris suggested that Jesus did not have a human mind; the divine *Logos* occupied the rational and willing aspects of His humanity. Apollinarianism was condemned at the First Council of Constantinople in AD 381 and again at Chalcedon in 451.

The obedience of Christ was not effortless. It was achieved in the face of opposition and temptation. He had to walk into the darkness, trusting in His Father's support. He needed the help of the Holy Spirit every step of the way. This suggests strongly that Jesus needed reassurance and confirmation of His identity and mission. And what better way to do it than to do something that Jesus had never before experienced in His incarnate humanity: a taste of glory!

Let Us Make Tents

It appears that up to this point, Peter, James, and John had been "heavy with sleep" (Luke 9:32) and had not witnessed the transfiguration or the appearance of Moses and Elijah. Awakening from their slumber, they witnessed Jesus' glory and His two companions. Peter called out: "Master, it is good that we are here. Let us make three tents, one for you and one for Moses and one for

Elijah" (v. 33). Luke adds the explanation that Peter did not know what he was saying. He spoke simply to prolong the moment.

Only Peter would say this! He had a propensity to say out loud whatever came into his mind. In today's jargon, he spoke "without a filter."

What could be better than this moment on the mountain? This is the greatest of all moments, and it should last forever—or at least a good, long season.

The suggestion to build tents for Jesus, Moses, and Elijah likely sprang from a desire to ensure that the good times lasted a long while. Peter had evidently not heard the conversation about Jesus' *departure*, a confirmation of Jesus' words a week earlier about His impending crucifixion being both true and necessary for the salvation of sinners. Perhaps Peter thought that Jesus would not need to suffer after all. Perhaps the kingdom had now come in its fullest form. Moses and Elijah had intervened.

But it wasn't only Jesus that Peter was thinking about. He was also thinking about himself and his two companions. "Master, it is good that *we* are here," he said (Luke 9:33, emphasis added).

Mountaintop experiences are the best. Being a disciple on the mountaintop was so much better than being a disciple in the valleys below. Today, Peter's confession at Caesarea Philippi was confirmed. Jesus was indeed the Christ, the Son of the living God. Good times have arrived!

Peter never forgot this moment. Many years later, shortly before his death, he wrote: "We were eyewitnesses of his majesty. For when he received honor and glory from God the Father, and the voice was borne to him by the Majestic Glory, 'This is my beloved Son, with whom I am well pleased,' we ourselves heard this very voice borne from heaven, for we were with him on the holy mountain" (2 Peter 1:16–18). Peter was an eyewitness of Jesus' *majesty*. He was there. One imagines that whenever Peter went to someone's home for dinner, people would ask him, "What do you remember most about Jesus?" In the early 60s, when Peter was in Rome, it was all too likely that no one in the city had ever seen Jesus. Peter was able to declare, "I was there on the holy mountain!"

He could have easily turned it into a traveling show and made some money from it. Instead, he makes less of it than being in possession of the written Word of God: "And we have the prophetic word more fully confirmed, to which you will do well to pay attention as to a lamp shining in a dark place, until the day dawns and the morning star rises in your hearts, knowing this first of all, that no prophecy of Scripture comes from someone's own interpretation. For no prophecy was ever produced by the will of man, but men spoke from God as they were carried along by the Holy Spirit" (2 Peter 1:19–21).

These are very significant words. Peter underlines the source of all authority: the Bible. Miracles and wonders such as the transfiguration had their place in confirming the identity of Jesus and the Apostles, but they were now events of the past and could not be witnessed by Peter's readers. But they had something more certain. Scripture is written by human authors ("*men spoke from God*"; v. 21, emphasis added), and these writers often reveal something of themselves in their writing style. At the same time, in a concurrent fashion, what these men wrote was entirely what God wanted them to write. They were "*carried along* by the Holy Spirit" (v. 21, emphasis added). Luke uses the same word, translated here as "carried along" (Greek, *pherō*), in Acts when he is describing Paul's shipwreck at sea: "And when the ship was caught and could not face the wind, we gave way to it and were *driven along*" (Acts 27:15, emphasis added; cf. Acts 27:17). Bible writers, including Peter, were driven along by the Spirit as they wrote.

Imagine the scenario in which you are asked which you would choose: being on the mountain with Jesus when He was transfigured or having a Bible in your hands. I wonder what your immediate reply would be. It is a test of just how important the Bible is to us.

The Glory Cloud

Just as Peter was speaking about making tents, the glory cloud appeared and enveloped them all. And then a voice said, "This is my Son, my Chosen One; listen to him!" (Luke 9:35).

The same voice had been heard before, at Jesus' baptism (3:22). The exhortation "listen to him" suggests that this voice was for Peter and the other two disciples. But it would also have been confirmation to Jesus at a moment when He needed it.

"My Chosen One." For Jesus, as well as the disciples, there was an echo of the first Servant Song of Isaiah 42:1:

Behold my servant, whom I uphold,
> my chosen, in whom my soul delights;

I have put my Spirit upon him.

There is a great deal of evidence that Jesus spent His entire life contemplating Isaiah's Servant Songs. If someone were asked to summarize Jesus' understanding of His own mission, a reasonable answer would point to Mark 10:45: "The Son of Man came not to be served but to serve, and to give his life as a ransom for many." "To serve . . . as a ransom for many." It is an echo of the fourth Servant Song: "He bore the sin of many" (Isa. 53:12). The very assurance of Jesus as the Chosen One was also a reminder that He would be led "like a lamb . . . to the slaughter" (v. 7).

Once the voice had spoken, Moses and Elijah disappeared, and "Jesus was found alone" (Luke 9:36).

What happened?

We are not told, but we imagine that they disappeared in the manner in which they had come. What if Jesus had gone away with them? What if Luke had written "and they were alone"? It is a terrifying thought, for had Jesus done so, there would be no salvation. We would forever remain in our sins, doomed to experience the wrath of God for eternity. The fact that Jesus was still there was a testimony to His resolve to see the plan of salvation through to its finish.

This had been an astonishing day, one that should have humbled Peter and his two companions. But a dozen verses later in Luke's account, we read that "an argument arose among them as to which of them was the greatest" (v. 46).

Imagine that!

Mountaintop experiences quickly fade.

Peter's Denial Predicted

The golfer Arnold Palmer recalled a lesson about overconfidence at the final hole of the 1961 Masters Tournament. He was one stroke ahead, and he hit a very fine tee shot. As he approached the ball, he saw an old friend in the gallery who motioned him over and stuck out his hand, adding a word of congratulations. Palmer took his hand and knew immediately that he had lost his focus. He hit the ball into the bunker. The next went over the green. He lost the Masters to the South African Gary Player. Later, Palmer mused, "You never forget a mistake like that, and you determine never to do it again."[1]

Overconfidence can get the better of us. And it was a hard lesson that Peter was to learn.

It is Passover. And it is the last week of Jesus' life. He and the disciples have gathered in the upper room, where Jesus initiates a celebration of the Lord's Supper (Luke 22:14–23). The disciples begin (again!) to argue about which one of them is the greatest (vv. 24–30; cf. 9:46–48).

Luke doesn't specifically single out Peter in either of these instances, but given what Jesus had said to him at Caesarea Philippi, it seems that the rest of the disciples might have been envious. And Peter, perhaps, had been less than humble. There is no report that Peter attempted to stop the unseemly quarrel. And considering the timing—it was the eve of Jesus' crucifixion—the spat has an element of brazen disregard for Jesus, who witnessed it.

At some point in the evening, Judas Iscariot slips away to fulfill his despicable role in the betrayal of Jesus to the authorities. In less than twenty-four hours, Jesus will be dead.

A Rooster at Dawn

Everyone heard it, which made it even more embarrassing. Jesus addressed Peter by his old name, Simon. It was the name he had used before Jesus initially called him. Jesus said, "Simon, Simon, behold, Satan demanded to have you" (Luke 22:31). It was an indication that what he was about to do reflected his past self.

To deny knowing Jesus at the hour of His greatest trial is cowardly, and Peter never thought for one single moment that he would fall victim to it. He thought of himself as better than that. The words of Jesus stung: "I tell you, Peter, the rooster will not crow this day, until you deny three times that you know me" (v. 34).

Before we examine the prophecy of Peter's denial, we need to look at something that has troubled Bible readers. How many rooster calls were heard at the time of Peter's denial? All the Synoptic Gospels relate the prophecy (Matt. 26:34; Mark 14:30; Luke 22:34). The problem arises in Mark's version: "Truly, I tell you, this very night, before the rooster crows *twice*, you will deny me three times" (Mark 14:30, emphasis added). And Mark also has two crows in the actual description of Peter's denial, once after the first denial and again after the third denial (vv. 68, 72). It is not surprising that some manuscripts omit Mark 14:68, "and the rooster crowed."

Roosters rarely crow just once. Typically, they crow two or three times, with a little interval between them. If, as in Peter's memory of it in his memoirs to Mark, there actually were two crows in Jesus' prediction and in the actual denial event, then we must interpret the single crowing in the other Gospels as more generic: "The rooster will not have finished his crowing until you deny Me three times."[2]

Was Peter capable of such a public denial? Evidently, Peter did not think so. He was ready to go with Jesus to prison and even to death (Luke 22:33). I think we should give Peter the benefit of the doubt that at the time he said this, he meant it with all his heart.

To be sure, Peter would experience both prison and death for Jesus. Just weeks later, he would be imprisoned with the Apostle John for preaching in the name of Jesus (Acts 4:3). And some thirty years later, he would be crucified, upside down, in Rome.

What lies behind this confidence of Peter's? It is *pride*, one of seven deadly sins. It is overconfidence in his own strength of will in the hour of temptation. Note that this is the second time that Peter has *corrected* Jesus. Peter had done so at Caesarea Philippi, when Jesus spoke of His crucifixion; Peter insisted that such a thing would never happen to Him. Evidently, Peter had not learned from Jesus' rebuke.

Solomon warns about the results of pride:

Pride goes before destruction,
> and a haughty spirit before a fall. (Prov. 16:18)

And it seems that Peter did too:

God opposes the proud but gives grace to the humble. (1 Peter 5:5)

Jonathan Edwards, in a lengthy treatment of undetected pride, suggested that evidence of it can be found in many ways, including faultfinding with others, overconcern with perceptions of oneself, and an inclination to be defensive when criticized.[3]

Satan's Desire

Just as Satan had been present in Caesarea Philippi, so he was present in this prophecy of Peter's downfall: "Simon, Simon, behold, Satan demanded to have you, that he might sift you like wheat" (Luke 22:31).

Demanded!

Nor was the temptation directed only at Peter; the "you" is plural. The rest of the disciples need to watch and learn.

As Jesus' death drew near, Satan's ire increased. What could he do to derail Jesus' mission? If he could not prevent Jesus from completing His atoning work, the next best (worst!) thing he could do was to humiliate Jesus' chief instrument in building the church, Peter, and bring disrepute on the entire plan (cf. Matt. 16:18).

Satan overreached. Perhaps he hoped that Peter would commit apostasy and never recover. As chief accuser, Satan desired to throw Peter into the air like wheat and watch him disintegrate.

What happens when Satan makes you his target? Realizing that we may be in the crosshairs of his malevolent designs is a very unsettling feeling. And Peter dwelled on it a great deal. He wrote: "Be sober-minded; be watchful. Your adversary the devil prowls around like a roaring lion, seeking someone to devour. Resist him, firm in your faith, knowing that the same kinds of suffering are being experienced by your brotherhood throughout the world" (1 Peter 5:8–9).

Never underestimate Satan's power to throw you off balance. Apart from the grace of God, there is no sin that we are incapable of doing. It is why we must pray and learn the Scriptures every day. It is why we must keep short accounts with God. It is why we need to be Spirit-filled every moment. It is why we need to wear and employ the whole armor of God (Eph. 6:10–20).

Why does God allow Satan the power to do what he did to Peter? We have no clear answer to that question. Satan is granted certain powers. He asked that he might test Job, and God permitted it (Job 1–2). Nowhere in the next forty chapters of Job are we given an explanation. Job had to trust that God knew what He was doing. But from another point of view, Satan's powers had clear boundaries that God Himself established. Initially, Satan could not lay a finger on Job himself, and in the second trial, he was granted permission to bring a terrible disease upon Job but had to stop short of death (1:12; 2:6).

Faced with the problem of evil, some theologians, such as Augustine of Hippo, speculated that the answer lay in what Augustine called *felix culpa*, the "happy fault." A universe that permits sin so that grace may be experienced is a better one than one in which sin is not permitted and grace is never experienced. Better a universe where Jesus becomes incarnate than one where He does not. This explanation does not answer all the problems with sin and evil or account for the sheer *amount* of evil, but it does seem to have some measure of sense in it.

Satan wants to make Christians turn away from their faith and their Lord. He wants to trip you. Peter wasn't the first, and he wasn't the last.

Perhaps, then, it is no surprise that trials are the very first subject that Peter raises in his first epistle:

Blessed be the God and Father of our Lord Jesus Christ! According to his great mercy, he has caused us to be born again to a living hope through the resurrection of Jesus Christ from the dead, to an inheritance that is imperishable, undefiled, and unfading, kept in heaven for you, who by God's power are being guarded through faith for a salvation ready to be revealed in the last time. In this you rejoice, though now for a little while, if necessary, you have been grieved by various trials, so that the tested genuineness of your faith—more precious than gold that perishes though it is tested by fire—may be found to result in praise and glory and honor at the revelation of Jesus Christ. (1 Peter 1:3–7)

Trials like the one that Peter faced tested the *genuineness* of his faith. Even if you fall, your inheritance is imperishable, undefiled, and unfading. God will keep you, through faith, and bring you to your everlasting salvation.

The Prayers of Jesus

There is no sweeter note in the warning of Satan's desire to "have" Peter and "sift [him] like wheat" (Luke 22:31) than the promise that Jesus attached to it: "But I have prayed for you that your faith may not fail" (v. 32a). It was as encouraging for Peter to hear Him promise His ongoing prayers for him as it is for us to read that Jesus continues to engage in intercessory prayer for us in heaven (Heb. 7:25).

John Murray summarizes the heavenly intercessory ministry of Christ this way:

The heavenly high priesthood of Christ means, therefore, that Christ appears in the presence of God at the right hand of the throne of the majesty in the heavens to present himself as the perfected high priest to plead on the basis of what he has accomplished the fulfilment of all the promises, the bestowment of all the benefits, and enduement with all the graces secured and ratified by his own high priestly offering. This is a ministry directed to the Father. This it is pre-eminently.[4]

Every Christian may entertain this assurance that Jesus is interceding on his or her behalf.

When trials abound, Jesus is praying for you.
When Satan is near, Jesus is praying for you.
When temptation is near, Jesus is praying for you.
When faith is weak, Jesus is praying for you.

In the hour of trial,
Jesus, pray for me,
lest by base denial
    I depart from Thee.
When Thou seest me waver,
    with a look recall,
nor for fear or favor
    suffer me to fall.

With its witching pleasures
    would this vain world charm,
or its sordid treasures
    spread to work me harm,
bring to my remembrance
    sad Gethsemane,
or, in darker semblance,
    cross-crowned Calvary.

If with sore affliction
    thou in love chastise,
pour thy benediction
    on the sacrifice:
then upon thine altar
    freely offered up,
though the flesh may falter,
    faith shall drink the cup.

When in dust and ashes
    to the grave I sink,
while heaven's glory flashes
    o'er the shelving brink,

on thy truth relying,
    through that mortal strife,
Lord, receive me, dying,
    to eternal life.[5]

There was also an exhortation for Peter, an exhortation that after the predicted denials he had a task to perform: "When you have turned again, strengthen your brothers" (Luke 22:32).

The fall was certain, but there is also the assurance of a rising again. And when that happens, Peter must be ready to help his fellow disciples. Who better to do that than one who has himself fallen? Perhaps that was Jesus' point. Jesus allowed Peter to fall to strengthen Peter by his recovery. He would be able to say to his fellow disciples: "I, too, know what fear means. I also know how weak I am in myself." Using the same word for "strengthen" (*stērizō*), Peter will himself reassure his frightened readers who faced Roman persecution that comfort is to be found in the knowledge that "after you have suffered a little while, the God of all grace, who has called you to his eternal glory in Christ, will himself restore, confirm, *strengthen*, and establish you" (1 Peter 5:10, emphasis added).

9

Peter's Denial

All four Gospels record Peter's denial (Matt. 26:69–75; Mark 14:66–72; Luke 22:55–62; John 18:15–18). Perhaps it was this failure by Peter that led him to exhort his readers, "[Be] prepared to make a defense to anyone who asks you for a reason for the hope that is in you" (1 Peter 3:15). Evidently, in the final hours of Jesus' life, Peter had not been prepared.

It was a failure of monumental proportions, public and life-changing. Every morning of Peter's life, he would hear a rooster crow and be reminded of his failure.

Peter loved Jesus with all his heart. In his mind, he was ready to die for Him (Luke 22:33). But when the time came, he flinched. Fear and self-preservation got the better of him, and he did the unthinkable. He did what he did not want to do. It is said that to be forewarned is to be forearmed, but evidently this is not always true. Despite Jesus' clear prediction, and Peter's disbelief, Peter flinched anyway. Studying the morphology of this collapse should be of some help to us, since we may face a similar moment in our pilgrimage.

Peter and the others had fallen asleep in Gethsemane while Jesus wrestled with the cost of what the Father had asked Him to do. In almost military fashion, Jesus had stationed Peter, James, and John near Him, as though needing their support in the hour of His trial. But they could not stay awake, and Jesus came to Peter, saying: "Simon, are you asleep? Could you not watch one hour? Watch and pray that you may not enter into temptation. The spirit indeed is willing, but the flesh is weak" (Mark 14:37–38). A second and a third time, Jesus found them sleeping. Had Peter forgotten the prediction that Jesus had made? Was he still of the opinion that Jesus was wrong? Did he not think that if ever there was a time to keep watch and pray, it was *now*? The spirit may well have been willing, but the flesh was weak. It always is.

Jesus' Arrest in Gethsemane

Then came Jesus' arrest. Judas had betrayed Him for a paltry thirty pieces of silver, and the deed would haunt Judas so much that he hanged himself after tossing the money onto the temple floor (Matt. 27:3–5).

In addition to Jewish officials (temple police), Judas also guided "a band of soldiers" to Jesus (John 18:3). The Greek (*tēn speiran*) suggests that they were not Jews but Roman auxiliaries. During feast days (it was Passover), these Romans were stationed in the fortress of Antonia to the northwest corner of the temple complex. They came bearing lanterns, torches, and weapons. And Judas led them straight to Jesus so that they might arrest Him.

One imagines a hundred or more soldiers in Gethsemane. There would have been no need to send the entire Roman auxiliary stationed at the fortress to arrest one unarmed man.

"Whom do you seek?" Jesus asks (John 18:4), at which point the soldiers fall to the ground (v. 6). Perhaps some of these soldiers had both seen and heard Jesus speak in the temple and are awed by His words (cf. 7:45–46). At the very least, they know Him to be a holy man with extraordinary powers. Replying to Jesus' question, the soldiers tell Him that they are looking for "Jesus of Nazareth" (18:5). There is a suggestion that the reply Jesus made, "I am he" (vv. 6, 8), would later have greater significance than it did to His immediate listeners. D.A. Carson points out that in Isaiah 40–55, it is God Himself who repeatedly takes these words on His lips.[1]

The scene is one of commotion. It is dark, and the terrain is hilly, with olive bushes in abundance. There is the prospect that the soldiers might arrest some of the disciples too. But Jesus intervenes and asks that all of them be released. Earlier, Jesus had prayed, "Of those whom you gave me I have lost not one" (John 18:9; cf. 17:12). But Peter is unnerved. He takes out his sword and cuts off the ear of the high priest's servant. John tells us that his name was Malchus (18:10). Luke, the doctor, is the only one who records that Jesus reaches out His finger, touches the servant's right ear, and heals him (Luke 22:51).

A question arises: Why was Peter carrying a sword? The Greek (*machaira*) may suggest that it was more like a small dagger rather than a military weapon. Did not Jesus' response to Peter that "all who take the sword will perish by the sword" (Matt. 26:52) suggest that Peter should not have been carrying one? Perhaps not. Carrying a knife or dagger to fillet a fish or cut some bread would have been a natural thing to do, as anyone who loves the outdoor life will attest. It is not the possession of the sword so much as its use as a weapon that Jesus addresses. It is not a ban on self-defense and certainly not a call to some form of pacifism. The history of Israel is riddled with acts of warfare. Jesus is simply making the point that if you live violently, you will probably die a violent death one day.

The Denials[2]

After His arrest, Jesus is taken first to Annas and his son-in-law, Caiaphas, the high priest. Caiaphas had said "it would be expedient that one man should die for the people" (John 18:14; cf. 11:51). It is not clear what Caiaphas meant when he said this, but he probably meant that a plot to kill Jesus would bring peace to the land. John, writing after the fact, draws attention to the fact that Caiaphas spoke more than he knew or realized. Jesus' death would indeed "gather into one the children of God who are scattered abroad" (11:52).

Peter and "another disciple" (probably John; see John 18:15) followed the soldiers to Annas and Caiaphas' residence. Peter, along with some others, was outside the courtyard, near a doorway that led into it. John was evidently inside the courtyard (Annas knew John) and went to fetch Peter and bring him inside (v. 16).

Standing[3] near a fire to warm himself (cf. Matt. 26:69), Peter was noticed by a servant girl, who said, "You also are not one of this man's disciples, are you?" (John 18:17; cf. Matt. 26:69; Luke 22:56). John refers to her as the doorkeeper (John 18:16). If John was known to Annas, John was probably known to the doorkeeper–servant girl. And if John was known as a disciple of Jesus, then Peter was also likely to be one. It seemed a reasonable inference. But Peter flatly denied it: "I am not" (v. 17).[4] And perhaps, if Peter had spoken while warming himself, his northern Galilean accent would become apparent, and it was well known that Jesus' disciples were all Galilean. This was his first denial. Jesus' prophecy was being fulfilled despite Peter's protests to the contrary.

Peter moved from where he was and headed toward the entrance, and Matthew records that "another" said, "This man was with Jesus of Nazareth"

(Matt. 26:71). The Greek for "another" (*allē*) is feminine, suggesting another servant girl.[5]

The third and final denial comes when "bystanders" (Matt. 26:73), among whom John singles out a servant of the high priest, a "relative of the man whose ear Peter had cut off," also exclaimed, "Did I not see you in the garden with him?" (John 18:26).[6] Again Peter denied the accusation. In Mark's account, Peter invoked a curse upon himself, swearing, "I do not know this man of whom you speak" (Mark 14:71).

At this point, John records, "at once a rooster crowed" (John 18:27).[7]

How the Mighty Have Fallen

It is a measure of the enormity of Peter's sin that he was not only a veteran disciple who had spent three years in Jesus' presence but also set apart as the chief Apostle in the building of Christ's church. He was not only one of the Twelve; he was Rocky, the number one Apostle. He had seen and heard more than most, and he had been chosen to see Jesus' transfiguration on the holy mountain. And still, he stumbled and fell. He had been warned that this would happen, and yet he failed to prevent it.

If this could happen to Peter, it could happen to every Christian. Each one of us is capable of any sin apart from the grace of God. Pride and fear pushed out courage and steadfastness. In the hour of trial, Peter failed to garner the strength of the Holy Spirit. He resorted to cowardice and petulance.

Peter denied Jesus *emphatically*. There is surely something symbolic in the fact that he did it *three* times. Three is always an assertive number. The threefold description of the Lord of hosts as "holy, holy, holy" in the vision Isaiah saw is designed to underline just how holy God is. And Peter's threefold denial is a way of saying that this was not just a small sin; it was colossal.

What brought it about? We have suggested fear and pride. But there was also Satan. Jesus had predicted as much: "Satan demanded to have you, that he might sift you like wheat" (Luke 22:31). Peter had been trapped in "the evil day" (Eph. 6:13). And he had failed to prepare for it. He carried a "sword" but failed to carry "the sword of the Spirit" (v. 17). He had failed to carry "the shield of faith, with which [he could] extinguish all the flaming darts of the evil one" (v. 16). Moreover, when he slept in the garden of Gethsemane, he failed to be at prayer "at all times in the Spirit, with all prayer and supplication" (v. 18).

No wonder, when the deed was done, with onlookers amazed at his cowardice, that Peter broke down and wept bitterly (Luke 22:62).

These were tears of shame, but they were also tears of regret. They would lead to repentance and renewal. Peter's pride needed to be broken. Every morning when the rooster crowed, Peter would remember this day.

This was Peter's lowest point, but high points lay ahead of him. Though he was a failure, Jesus was not finished with him. Jesus was not about to cast Peter aside. There was work for him to do.

The only way for Peter to go from this low point was upward.

10

He Appeared to Cephas

We left Peter in tears after his threefold denial of Jesus. That was early Friday morning. Since then, it isn't at all clear where Peter had been. Perhaps he had gone to hide. Perhaps to reflect. Perhaps to pray. But by Sunday morning, he is with John, heading toward a tomb on the outskirts of the city.

After the trial with Annas, Caiaphas, and Pilate, Jesus was sentenced to death by crucifixion. The charge under Roman law was treason. Despite Pilate's prevarications, Jesus had made Himself King. Worse, He had blasphemed by claiming to be the Son of God. Pilate's hands were tied, and Jesus was sentenced to be tortured and crucified. By midafternoon that Friday, He was dead.

He died relatively quickly. Crucifixions sometimes took days to kill their victims. It seems that once Jesus had paid the price for our sins, His Father saw to it that the trajectory would be upward. A soldier pierced His side to prove that He was dead, and given that the Sabbath would begin at dusk, Jesus was taken down and given a hasty burial in a borrowed tomb of Joseph of Arimathea. Nicodemus came with seventy-five pounds of spices to temporarily anoint His body until a proper burial could be given Him on Sunday morning when the Sabbath was over (John 19:38–39).

John had witnessed Jesus' death, as had Jesus' mother, Mary. From the cross, Jesus had asked John to care for Mary as if she were his own mother and Mary to regard John as though he were her own son (John 19:25–27). Two other women named Mary were also present: Mary the wife of Clopas and

Mary Magdalene. If these witnesses with personal ties to Jesus weren't enough, the professional soldiers, who had likely witnessed hundreds of crucifixions, could also verify Jesus' death.

It is not clear whether Peter witnessed the crucifixion. Luke tells of a crowd that had gathered and, seeing the crucifixion, "returned home beating their breasts." Then he adds, "And all [Jesus'] acquaintances and the women who had followed him from Galilee stood at a distance watching these things" (Luke 23:48–49). Was Peter one of these? If he was, it would make sense that he stood at a distance, given the events of that morning.

Jesus' body was bound in linen cloths packed with a very large amount of spices. Joseph of Arimathea, a secret disciple, rolled the huge stone down an inclined trough to close the tomb (Matt. 27:60). Mary Magdalene and "the other Mary" (Mark identifies her as "the mother of Joses"; Mark 15:47) sat nearby, watching Joseph of Arimathea close the tomb (Matt. 27:61).

On Saturday, the Sabbath, the chief priests and the Pharisees went to Pilate, insisting that a guard be placed at the tomb to prevent Jesus' disciples from stealing away the body and claiming a resurrection. Pilate agreed. The tomb was sealed, and a guard was placed outside it (Matt. 27:62–66).

These details are important to rebuff the notion that Jesus wasn't dead but simply unconscious, and that He revived later in the cool temperatures of the tomb, or that the disciples stole the body sometime on Saturday evening.

An Unexpected Event

It is a very surprising discovery that no one was expecting Jesus to rise from the dead. Not the women. Not the disciples. Not Peter. The only ones who thought Jesus' resurrection was a possibility were Jesus' enemies, and even they didn't believe in an actual resurrection. Instead, they feared that Jesus' disciples might undertake some trickery and invent a story of resurrection.

It is quite common for antisupernaturalists to mock the story of the resurrection of Christ by suggesting that first-century folk were primitive and gullible enough to believe in the resurrection because *they were expecting it*. The expectation invented the narrative. But the very opposite is true. First-century folk knew all too well that deceased people do not rise from the dead.

Early that Sunday morning, Mary Magdalene set out, "while it was still dark"[1] (John 20:1), to anoint Jesus' body after the hasty burial on Friday ahead of the Sabbath. Though John's gospel mentions only Mary Magdalene, other Gospels add that she was not alone. Among her companions were Mary the mother of James, Salome, and Joanna (cf. Matt. 28:1; Mark 16:1; Luke 24:10). Later, John will record Mary Magdalene as saying, after discovering that the tomb was empty, "*We* do not know where they have laid him" (John 20:2, emphasis added).

How these women were going to roll back the heavy stone is not clear. Some conjecture that it might take a dozen men to roll the stone back up the grooved incline. Perhaps Mary figured that the guards might do that for her.

As she enters the garden, remembering the location of the tomb from less than thirty-six hours earlier, Mary sees that the stone has been "taken away from the tomb" (John 20:1). And she runs to fetch Peter and "the other disciple" (John; v. 2) to tell them that someone has opened the tomb. Her instinct was not to go inside the tomb but to let Peter and John know that grave robbers have been at work.

Peter and John run to the tomb, and John reaches the tomb first. It is as Mary has said. The stone has been removed, and John peers inside, seeing "the linen cloths lying there" (v. 5). This is no grave robbery! Robbers would hardly take the time to remove Jesus' body from the linen cloths or leave behind expensive material and seventy-five pounds of equally precious spices. Something has happened here, but what?

Peter arrives, and while John is peering into the tomb, Peter steps inside, noticing details that only an eyewitness would describe. "He saw the linen cloths lying there, and the face cloth, which had been on Jesus' head, not lying with the linen cloths but folded up in a place by itself" (vv. 6–7). John follows Peter and sees the same thing. The only explanation for what John sees is a resurrection; Jesus' body, somehow, some way, had come to life and passed through these linen cloths. Jesus carefully folded the cloth that had been around His head in a place by itself. Lazarus, John would recall, had come out of his tomb still wrapped in cloths (11:44).

Up until now, John had not understood Jesus' claim that He would rise from the dead, but standing in the empty tomb, "he saw and believed" (20:8–9).

I Am Ascending to My Father and Your Father

It had been the longest Sabbath ever. Especially for Peter. The events of the last week, especially Thursday evening and Friday, surely drained the disciples of all energy. They feared for their lives. On Saturday evening, they were in the home of John Mark and his mother, Salome, "the doors being locked . . . for fear of the Jews" (John 20:19).

But now, the unthinkable has happened, and Peter and John return to their lodgings in the city to tell the other disciples. Evidently, they did not come across Mary Magdalene, now making her way back to the tomb for the second time, or else they would have informed her of their belief in the resurrection.

When Mary Magdalene arrives at the tomb once more, she sees two angels in white, sitting where the body of Jesus had been. Angels appear at all the important redemptive moments. Noticing that she is crying, they ask her, "Woman, why are you weeping?" (v. 13). And she responds, telling the same tale of body snatchers and grave robbers. Turning around, she sees someone standing in the opening of the tomb. This person once more asks: "Woman, why are you weeping? Whom are you seeking?" Thinking He was the gardener, she said to Him, "Sir, if you have carried him away, tell me where you have laid him, and I will take him away" (vv. 14–15).

I wonder whether John is thinking, as he narrates this account: "Mary, He *is* the Gardener, but not the one that you think. He has come to restore this world and make it like Eden!" Only when she hears Him call out her name does she perceive His identity. It is Jesus! And she clings to Him, only for Jesus to remind her that He has not yet ascended but that He will ultimately do so. She must go to Jesus' "brothers," the disciples, and tell them this message from Jesus: "I am ascending to my Father and your Father, to my God and your God" (John 20:17).

These words of Jesus to Mary Magdalene are deeply significant. It is an affirmation that we have the same heavenly Father as Jesus did. And more pertinently, the same God. Yes, in His human nature, and even in His *resurrected* human nature, He addressed His heavenly Father as "God." Christians belong to a family in which Jesus is our Elder Brother.

The Meeting

If Peter was not present at the crucifixion, the last time Peter had seen Jesus was at the time of his threefold denial. Luke specifically points out that at the moment of the third denial, "the Lord turned and looked at Peter" (Luke 22:61). Peter had not had time to express his remorse to Jesus. Peter had not asked for forgiveness.

Now Jesus is alive, but where is He? Will Peter have a moment when he can be reconciled to his Savior?

None of the Gospels record Peter's first encounter with the resurrected Jesus. Even Mark's gospel, based, it is believed, on Peter's memoirs, bears no record of it. Instead, Paul mentions it in an almost offhand comment in his great chapter on the resurrection in 1 Corinthians: "And . . . he appeared to Cephas" (15:5). It must have occurred before the occasion when Jesus showed Himself to the ten disciples (Thomas was absent) later that day.

We do not know where or precisely when this meeting with the resurrected Jesus took place. In all probability, it was after He appeared to Cleopas and the other disciple on the road to Emmaus (Mark 16:12–13; Luke 24:13–32).

It was all very embarrassing for Peter, and there were probably expressions of joy mixed with grief. Perhaps the incident was so deeply personal that we were not meant to pry into the painful restoration of a fallen brother. This was between Peter and Jesus.

I am certain that Jesus did not make it hard for Peter. Having expressed his sorrow, Peter was forgiven. The blood spilled on Calvary ensured that. Plus, there was work for Peter to do, and he needed to get himself ready for it. Just as there is work to do for all of God's fallen children who walk back into His arms with repentant hearts.

A Bad Conscience

The resurrection was central in Peter's thinking. He mentions it in the very opening verses of his first epistle: "Blessed be the God and Father of our Lord Jesus Christ! According to his great mercy, he has caused us to be born again to a living hope through the resurrection of Jesus Christ from the dead" (1 Peter 1:3). Our hope of everlasting life is based in the resurrection of Jesus Christ. It is not the cross that Peter mentions but the resurrection. The cross is vital. Without it, there is no forgiveness of sins. There is no atonement. There is no payment of a ransom price. There is no satisfaction of divine justice. But in the resurrection, there is testimony to the fact that the cross has achieved what it set out to do. Without it, there is no "Well done, good and faithful servant" (Matt. 25:21, 23).

One further text in 1 Peter signals the theological importance of the resurrection of Christ. And it is not an easy text to unravel: "Baptism, which corresponds to this, now saves you, not as a removal of dirt from the body but as an appeal to God for a good conscience, through the resurrection of Jesus Christ" (1 Peter 3:21). The passage is notoriously difficult, and all its nuances need not detain us here. At the heart of it lies the thought that the resurrection of Christ is the *only* way that Christians may have a "good conscience."

Peter knew all about a bad conscience. Those hours after his denial were filled with remorse. A bad conscience destroys all spiritual life. It saps energy and quenches all hope. But the resurrection is the guarantee that the Father approves the finished work of Christ on behalf of sinners. It is the visible expression that even a sinner such as Peter may entertain a good conscience in the presence of the risen Jesus.

And so may every Christian enjoy such hope.

Come, ye weary, heavy laden,
    bruised and broken by the fall;
If you tarry 'til you're better,
    you will never come at all:
not the righteous, not the righteous—
    sinners Jesus came to call.

Let not conscience make you linger,
    nor of fitness fondly dream;
All the fitness he requireth
    is to feel your need of him;
this he gives you, this he gives you—
    'tis the Spirit's rising beam.

Lo! Th'incarnate God, ascended,
    pleads the merit of his blood;
venture on him; venture wholly,
    let no other trust intrude:
none but Jesus, none but Jesus
    can do helpless sinners good.[2]

11

Gone Fishing!

After Jesus' private appearance to Peter, Jesus appeared to ten of the disciples (Thomas, for some reason, was not there) and commissioned them for service in the kingdom of God, saying, "As the Father has sent me, even so I am sending you" (John 20:21). To aid them in this task, He declared to them, "Receive the Holy Spirit" (v. 22).

A week later, when the weeklong Feast of Unleavened Bread concluded, Jesus appeared to the disciples again, this time with Thomas—*doubting Thomas.* Jesus instructed him: "Put your finger here, and see my hands; and put out your hand, and place it in my side. Do not disbelieve, but believe" (v. 27). Whether Thomas did what Jesus asked, we are not told, but we are told that Thomas believed, exclaiming, "My Lord and my God!" (v. 28). Peter witnessed these two appearances, learning that he was not the only one who faltered when the time came to confess Christ. It had been a time when Satan had demanded to sift them as wheat and they had failed to resist him and stand firm in their faith (cf. 1 Peter 5:9).

When the Passover and Unleavened Bread festivities were over, it was time to go home. John does not tell us exactly when they left Jerusalem ("after this"; John 21:1) or whether they went in small groups of two or three or with the crowds leaving Jerusalem heading north.

Peter should have known that there would be at least one more appearance of the risen Jesus ahead of them. Predicting Peter's denial, Jesus had said: "You will all fall away, for it is written, 'I will strike the shepherd, and the sheep will be scattered.' But after I am raised up, I will go before you to Galilee"

(Mark 14:27–28). Later, the eleven disciples will go to the mountain where Jesus will deliver the Great Commission (Matt. 28:16–20).

But what was Peter to do now? The answer, it seems, was to go back to his day job. Finding himself with several of the other disciples, he told them, "I am going fishing" (John 21:3).

On the surface, the statement sounds innocent enough. Fishing was Peter's business, as it was for Andrew and the sons of Zebedee. He and the others had been gone for some time, and it was now time to return to their fishing business.

Was Peter still smarting from his downfall? Was he, perhaps, still nursing the thought that he had failed at being a disciple and that the only thing for him to do now was what he knew he was good at: *fishing*? That would make him feel better. The Sea of Galilee had provided Peter and his business companions with a steady income, something they may have needed to replenish given their long periods of absence.

They fished all night. And John summarizes the fruitless result: "That night they caught nothing" (John 21:3). Their nets repeatedly came up empty.

One can imagine the frustration in Peter's heart. He had failed as a disciple, and now he was failing at being a fisherman. This was one of those "various trials" moments (1 Peter 1:6). When Jesus wants you to be a full-time disciple, doing what He commands, He will make sure that if you try to do something else, you will come up empty. Peter's fishing-business days were in the past; he was now called to be what Jesus told him the very first time they met: *a fisher of men* (Mark 1:17).

Stranger on the Shore

At dawn, they were aware of a stranger on the shore who called out, "Children, do you have any fish?" (John 21:5). The monosyllabic answer was no. We may be reading too much into the response, but given the frustration of the night's labors and the lack of sleep, the terse response may have been yet another expression of the futility of it all. They definitely were not in the mood for a conversation and, even less, to receive fishing instructions from a complete stranger. Imagine their annoyance when Jesus told them, "Cast the net on the right side of the boat, and you will find some" (v. 6).

But they did it anyway, and suddenly they felt the familiar tug in their nets suggesting not just some fish but a large catch, so much so that they were finding it difficult to haul their nets into the boat (v. 6).

It was John who recognized the identity of the stranger on the shore. "It is the Lord!" John said. Peter, stripped for fishing, put on his outer garment and jumped into the sea. The boat was out at sea sufficiently far that Peter would have had to swim until he reached the shallower waters at the shore. The other disciples rowed the boat to the coastline, dragging their catch of fish behind them (vv. 7–8).

When Peter and the rest of the disciples were on land, they noticed that Jesus had made Himself a charcoal fire and was cooking some fish on it. Were these fish for Himself? The fact that He asks the disciples to bring *additional* fish from their catch suggests that He hadn't prepared food for them and that this breakfast likely was for Him. Had He caught them? And if so, how? These questions are not answered for us. Nevertheless, it is a testimony to the reality of Jesus' resurrection body that when He first appeared to the ten disciples (Thomas was not there), He asked them, "Have you anything here to eat?" Luke tells us that they gave Jesus a piece of broiled fish to eat (Luke 24:41–42). Clearly, as John meticulously points out, here in Galilee Jesus ate breakfast too: "Jesus came and took the bread and gave it to them, and so with the fish" (John 21:13).

We should pause and reflect on the significance of these twofold references to Jesus' eating in His resurrected body.

The Bible suggests that there are areas of continuity and discontinuity in our experience of life in this world and life in the next. Our future existence, in the new heavens and new earth, is certainly a physical one. It will include biology, physiology, and, in my understanding, space and time. As for eating, I have written on this elsewhere. Some of what I wrote bordered on the speculative side, but I think we can be allowed some sanctified speculation if its roots are in Scripture. This is what I wrote:

> Take the matter of eating and drinking. Paul sees the resurrection of Jesus as a model for own future resurrection: "as we have borne the image of the man of dust, we shall also bear the image of the man of heaven" (1 Cor. 15:49). Jesus' resurrection body is the "firstfruits" (1 Cor. 15:20). His current body is more than a guarantee of our future resurrection; it provides the *template* for own future body.

Jesus ate fish cooked on a charcoal fire in His resurrected body beside the Sea of Galilee (Luke 24:40–43; John 21:1–19). And while it may be true that further changes in Jesus' body take place from resurrected to ascended state, the Bible does not specifically say so. Can we therefore conjecture (and for now, conjecture is what it is) that our future existence will include eating? After all, the future form of the kingdom is described in terms of a banquet (Luke 14:16–24), or a wedding meal (Rev. 19:9). And, at the inauguration of the Lord's Supper, Jesus said, "I tell you I will not drink again of this fruit of the vine until that day when I drink it new with you in my Father's kingdom" (Matt. 26:29; Mark 14:25).

And what about eating meat in the resurrected body, as Jesus did? Meat-eating is first mentioned *after* the Flood (Gen. 9:3), suggesting to many that before the Flood human beings were vegetarian. Should we therefore assume that in a redeemed universe, human beings will revert to a vegetarian diet? The logic seems flawed if we follow the example of Jesus after His resurrection. To some, the very thought of killing is wrong; but to others, killing for the sake of food is ethically justifiable. And *if* we follow the logic, will we hunt in the new world? Having never enjoyed the experience here, I find it difficult to imagine it there; but is it altogether out of the question? Will there really be "No Fishing" signs on every pool and lake and river? The logic gets complicated: how will the depletion of fish be remedied? In the next chapter, we will address the statement (by Jesus) about no marriage in heaven. And presumably, no sex. And therefore, no procreation. No babies will be born in the new earth. Will this also be true of animals and birds, and fish? Our minds begin to reel at the complexity of this line of thought.[1]

The Measurement of the Fish

When the disciples brought their catch of fish ashore, they counted 153 fish. Archimedes, the great Greek mathematician, pointed out the significance of the number 153, associating it with the geometric shape known as Vesica Piscis or Mandorla.[2] Also, if you add all the numbers from 1 to 17, the total is 153. The number 153 is, therefore, the seventeenth "triangular number." Scholars have speculated that John, who has a fascination with numbers in the book of Revelation, wants us to see some significance in pointing out that there were 153 fish. In technical terms, is John employing a form of Jewish gematria, intending to signify some hidden meaning?[3] And if so, what? Perhaps John is simply trying to tell us that there were a *lot* of fish!

Lessons were given that morning on the shore of the Sea of Galilee. First, as we have already pointed out, if we try to do what Jesus doesn't want us to do, nothing will come of it.

Second, before Peter could be fully restored, his pride had to be dealt with. Peter had been forgiven. But forgiveness is not restoration, and if it takes another lesson in humility, so be it. Peter still had a label on his outer garment that read, "Will not shrink," and Jesus is determined to shrink it.

Shrinking pride is painful and embarrassing. And Peter experienced both pain and embarrassment.

It is not clear whether what followed was in the presence of all the fishermen or somewhere apart for Peter alone to hear. Since it has to do with addressing Peter's public denial, it may well have been for others to overhear too.

"Do you love me more than these?" Jesus asked Peter (John 21:15). It was an important question, but also an embarrassing one. The fact that Jesus asked him suggested that there might be some doubt about it, doubt cast not by Peter's affection (earlier, he had jumped into the Sea of Galilee without thinking in his desire to be near Jesus again) but by his recent denials. Those public denials were serious and a blot on his character, and they suggested a lack of love for Jesus. Jesus needed his love in the hour of His trial more than at any other time, and Peter had let Him down. It was now time to face the truth.

Jesus asked Peter *three* times, reflecting the threefold denial. Peter understood the reason for these three questions.

Scholars have pointed out that in the first two instances Jesus employs the same word for "love" (*agapaō*) but that in the third instance He uses a different word (*phileō*). Is there some significance? And in Peter's response, he consistently uses what some view as the *weaker* verb, *phileō*. Is it because Peter has been so shaken by his failure that he cannot bring himself to use the stronger *agapaō*?[4] Others are far less convinced and argue that the two verbs are used interchangeably in the gospel of John. And even more to the point, Jesus and Peter were speaking Aramaic, not Greek, where the subtlety would not apply. Perhaps John, in writing the account years later, simply wanted to introduce some variation of vocabulary.[5]

Each response by Peter was followed by a command:

"Feed my lambs." (John 21:15)
"Tend my sheep." (v. 16)
"Feed my sheep." (v. 17)

Again, the variation of words has made some search for nuanced differences in what Jesus was asking Peter to do, but that seems a little strained. What is certain is that when Jesus leaves their immediate presence, Peter will be responsible for watching over the flock of God. He must be their shepherd, an undershepherd of "the great shepherd of the sheep" (Heb. 13:20).

Concluding his first letter, Peter seems to recall this moment when he addresses fellow elders: "So I exhort the elders among you, as a fellow elder and a witness of the sufferings of Christ, as well as a partaker in the glory that is going to be revealed: shepherd the flock of God that is among you, exercising oversight, not under compulsion, but willingly, as God would have you; not for shameful gain, but eagerly; not domineering over those in your charge, but being examples to the flock. And when the chief Shepherd appears, you will receive the unfading crown of glory" (1 Peter 5:1–4).

Intimation of Peter's Death

Before the breakfast was over, Jesus said something sobering and painful. It was a prophecy about the manner of Peter's death: "'Truly, truly, I say to you, when you were young, you used to dress yourself and walk wherever you wanted, but when you are old, you will stretch out your hands, and another will dress you and carry you where you do not want to go.' (This he said to show by what kind of death he was to glorify God.)" (John 21:18–19).

Peter might not have understood it completely. It is unlikely that he did. And John's parenthetical comment explaining to his readers that Jesus was talking about Peter's death was written decades later. There was sufficient ambiguity about what Jesus said to Peter that the statement required a fuller explanation. Peter was to follow Jesus to his death, a violent one at that, crucified upside down (at his own request, so that he would not be compared to his Savior).

Then Jesus bid Peter to follow Him, and it seems that John was behind them. Peter asked whether John, too, was to die in the same manner, but Jesus declined to answer, adding, "What is that to you?" (v. 22). That comparison would only lead Peter in a direction that would not help him obey what Jesus was asking him to do.

Peter must concern himself with the task before him and not compare his lot with others. He must obey and do his work well.

The time had come to stop comparisons with other people's lives.

The time had come for Peter to show his mettle and to look to Jesus and follow Him submissively and dutifully.

12

Pentecost

There was one more sighting of Jesus at which Peter was present. It occurred at a mountain in Galilee (perhaps the Mount of Transfiguration) just before the ascension of Jesus into heaven. It was the occasion of the Great Commission.

Matthew records that "the eleven disciples went to Galilee, to the mountain to which Jesus had directed them" (Matt. 28:16). Astonishingly, despite previous resurrection appearances, there remained some doubt among a few of the disciples (v. 17). Reminding them of His absolute authority in heaven and on earth, Jesus commissioned them to go and make disciples, adding two aspects of what discipleship might mean: they were to baptize them in the Trinitarian name of God (an ecclesiastical dimension), and they were to teach them to observe all that Jesus had commanded (a pedagogical dimension) (vv. 18–20).

Neither Matthew nor John records the ascension. Mark summarizes it in one sentence but gives no account as to when and where it took place (Mark 16:19). Luke records it twice, once at the close of his gospel and then again in the opening chapter of Acts (Luke 24:50–53; Acts 1:6–11). In Luke's gospel, the ascension takes place in Bethany,[1] on the Mount of Olives, two miles or so from Jerusalem. Evidently, after the Great Commission in the north, the disciples came back to Jerusalem. Pentecost, which follows this event, is six weeks after Passover.

Peter was present when the disciples asked Jesus, "Lord, will you at this time restore the kingdom to Israel?" (Acts 1:6). John Calvin famously observed, "There are as many errors in this question as there are words."[2] Others have been less critical.[3] It does appear that their myopic focus on "Israel" was not yet corrected by what Pentecost would bring, confirming the *international* aspect of gospel focus. Moreover, the question demonstrates that they also seemed to be expecting Jesus to begin His kingly reign on earth *right then*. But that was not Jesus' immediate intention, and Peter heard Jesus speak of receiving "power" when the Holy Spirit came upon the disciples; Jesus added, "You will be my witnesses in Jerusalem and in all Judea and Samaria, and to the end of the earth" (Acts 1:8).

And then Jesus was gone. He "was lifted up, and a cloud took him out of their sight" (v. 9). Peter had been in Jesus' presence for the last three years, among His innermost circle. But now Jesus had disappeared, and Peter would not see Him in this world again.

Returning to Jerusalem, Peter immediately takes charge, fulfilling the role that Jesus gave him. After Judas Iscariot's departure, the disciples were only eleven. They needed to be twelve again. Quoting from two psalms, 69 and 109, Peter drew on two prophecies, one predicting the betrayal of Judas Iscariot and another that said, "Let another take his office." Two candidates were singled out: Joseph (also called Justus) and Matthias. Casting lots, they chose Matthias (Acts 1:15–26). They were twelve again.

It was Scripture, not expediency, that governed Peter's actions. It was a sign of things to come. It is highly unlikely that Peter had the scrolls of the book of Psalms with him, and it is a testimony to his piety that he quoted these psalms from memory. He understood that everything was now different. Jesus' departure into heaven meant that the disciples were alone. And yet they were not, for Jesus had spoken several times of the Holy Spirit's coming upon and empowering them. It was time to see what Jesus meant.

A Mighty Rushing Wind

When Pentecost[4] arrived, the disciples "were all together in one place" somewhere in the temple's outer courts (Acts 2:1). And "suddenly" the Holy Spirit descended (v. 2). It was an event difficult for Luke to describe; it was "*like* a mighty rushing wind," and "divided tongues *as of* fire" appeared and rested on them (vv. 2–3, emphasis added).

It is not clear in English, but in Hebrew and Greek, the words for "wind," "breath," and "spirit/Spirit" are the same. This event brought memories of Ezekiel 37, where God summons the Spirit over the valley of dry bones: "Come from the four winds, O breath, and breathe on these slain, that they may live" (v. 9). It also was a reminder that at the very beginning of creation, the Spirit of God hovered over the waters (Gen. 1:2). A *new* creation was taking place (cf. 2 Cor. 5:17).

The fiery tongues were also a reminder of the presence of God, the pillar of fire that had led Israel through the wilderness, encouraging God's people of His presence and protection but at the same time representing a threat to His enemies (Ex. 13:21–22). And the fact that these fiery tongues rested on each one individually was also significant, showing that the presence of God was no longer localized in the temple but was indwelling every believer. Each believer is the temple of the living God (1 Cor. 6:19). Later, when Peter counseled those Christians facing the hostile insults of the world, he exhorted them to rejoice "because the Spirit of glory and of God rests upon [them]" (1 Peter 4:14).

Why, especially, *tongues*? Because each disciple was given the ability to speak in a language that he did not previously know.[5] Why? Because present at Pentecost were thousands of Diaspora Jews, "Parthians and Medes and Elamites and residents of Mesopotamia, Judea and Cappadocia, Pontus and Asia, Phrygia and Pamphylia, Egypt and the parts of Libya belonging to Cyrene, and visitors from Rome, both Jews and proselytes, Cretans and Arabians" (Acts 2:9–11). These were Jews who now spoke different languages. And for them to understand what was taking place, they needed to hear the message in their own native languages.

Nothing could more perfectly signal the fact that the gospel was no longer confined to a small piece of land in the Middle East than the international, multilingual message at this Pentecost celebration. The doors were now wide open to build Christ's church from every tribe, tongue, and nation. The Great Commission had urged the disciples to go into *all the world*, and Pentecost was the signal that the time to do so was *now*.

A New Peter

A new Peter emerges, strong and forceful, with a power and conviction that we have only partially seen. Something has filled him with courage and faith. *Someone* has filled him. This is Peter filled with the Holy Spirit (cf. Acts 2:4).

The sermon that Peter preaches, the first of many, is both astonishing in its depth and breathtaking in its use of the Old Testament. He was a fisherman, but even before he met Christ, he was devout and thoughtful. He had memorized large sections of the Old Testament, and he had listened carefully to the way in which Jesus used the Scriptures. In the last three years, Peter had been in the best peripatetic seminary that the world has ever witnessed. His Teacher was Jesus.

Examining Peter's Pentecost sermon, what do we find?

First, there is Peter's understanding of the redemptive message of the Old Testament. He views the entire Old Testament as a preparation for this moment. He is able to bring the entire narrative together as one essential message of salvation.

Rabbis referred to three main sections of the Hebrew Bible: the Torah, consisting of the five books of Moses, also known as the Pentateuch; the Nevi'im, or the Prophets; and the Ketuvim, or Writings.[6] For Peter, these three sections, including the individual books, expressed *one* message: God intended to save His people from their sins through His Son, Jesus Christ. Peter shows a conviction that what he experienced at Pentecost was the fulfillment of what God had been saying for centuries.

Peter points to the prophet Joel and a lengthy prophecy in Joel 2 from which Peter quotes (from memory) at length, adding, "This is that" (Acts 2:16, KJV). In effect, Peter is saying, "What you see happening here today is what the prophet spoke about centuries ago."[7] Peter changes Joel's "afterward" to "in the last days" (v. 17). From Joel's point of view, it was later, but from Peter's point of view, *it is now*. And significantly, the coming of the Spirit at Pentecost has ushered in "the last days."

Pentecost changes how we view time. The coming of the Holy Spirit is a declaration that we are in the "last days" (cf. Heb. 1:2). This does not imply that Peter thought that there were just months or even a few years left. What he meant was that the next great redemptive event (whenever that will be) will be the second coming and the ushering in of the new heavens and new earth. Peter would later tell his readers, "But according to his promise we are waiting for new heavens and a new earth in which righteousness dwells" (2 Peter 3:13).

In a dramatic twist that devout Jews must surely have caught, Peter identifies the One upon whom they must call in order to be saved as "Lord" (Acts

2:21–23). In the Hebrew text of Joel 2:32, it is the divine name "LORD" (the divine name Yahweh). Peter is making the connection that Yahweh is Jesus!

Second, Peter demonstrates a grasp of providence. As he ponders the events of the last six weeks, from the crucifixion, resurrection, and ascension of Jesus, he sees God's hand at work. These were not simply haphazard events with no particular meaning. They were all orchestrated by God.

Possessing a clear grasp of the doctrine of divine providence provides for a powerful faith. Speaking of the death of Jesus six weeks earlier, Peter proclaims a breathtaking point of view: "Men of Israel, hear these words: Jesus of Nazareth, a man attested to you by God with mighty works and wonders and signs that God did through him in your midst, as you yourselves know—this Jesus, delivered up according to the definite plan and foreknowledge of God, you crucified and killed by the hands of lawless men. God raised him up, loosing the pangs of death, because it was not possible for him to be held by it" (Acts 2:22–24).

Who killed Jesus? It was "lawless men," and specifically "you," referring to some of the Jews present. But at the same time, Jesus was "delivered up according to the definite plan and foreknowledge of God" (v. 23). Men did it. God did it. In what we refer to today as a compatibilist understanding of the nature of divine causality, God orchestrates the details of history without being the author of sin. There is man's responsibility and there is God's sovereignty. And Peter refuses to compromise either.

God has a plan. In times when the world seems crazy, it is a good thing to know that God has a plan and that He intends to make it happen.

Third, Peter has a conviction about the identity of Jesus as Lord of history. He was a man attested "by God with mighty works and wonders and signs that God did through him in [their] midst" (Acts 2:22). This Jesus had been killed, only to be resurrected three days later. "God raised him up," Peter declares (v. 24). Death could not hold on to Him. Quoting from Psalm 16, Peter draws attention to some words about the resurrection. The prevailing interpretation at the time was that these referred to the resurrection of David. But David is dead, and his tomb is a five-minute walk away from where they stood (Acts 2:29). David was not talking about himself in Peter's quoting of David as saying, "You will not abandon my soul to Hades" (v. 27, quoting Ps. 16:10). David was talking about Jesus' resurrection.

Peter also quotes the opening verse of Psalm 110: "The Lord said to my Lord, 'Sit at my right hand, until I make your enemies your footstool'" (Acts 2:34–35, quoting Ps. 110:1), adding, "Let all the house of Israel therefore know for certain that God has made him both Lord and Christ, this Jesus whom you crucified" (Acts 2:36). At that point, many were "cut to the heart," asking Peter and the rest of the Apostles, "Brothers, what shall we do?" (v. 37).

There was only one thing for them to do: repent and be baptized. Forgiveness of sins is possible, but only through faith in Christ. Sinners need to be in union with Christ, symbolized by baptism as a sign and seal to faith of all that the gospel offers (v. 38).

And they needed to do so with haste! They needed to save themselves "from this crooked generation" (v. 40).

And many of them believed. Luke records that "three thousand souls" received Peter's word and were baptized (v. 41).

An evangelist awoke at Pentecost, with a sense of urgency and conviction. By the grace of God, Peter now seems to be a new man. And a Jesus movement began, made up mostly of Jewish believers in Christ, not yet called "Christians" and not yet gathering in churches. There was a great deal to learn and a great deal to do.

13

Repent

Peter is a changed man. Filled with the Holy Spirit, he has preached an extraordinary sermon on the day of Pentecost, when "about three thousand souls" were added to the roll of believers (Acts 2:41).

Days pass, and these new believers devote themselves to the Apostles' "teaching and the fellowship, to the breaking of bread and the prayers" (v. 42). This suggests that the fledgling church was studying the Scriptures under the direction of the Apostles, encouraging one another in mutual love and support, sharing together (the key meaning of "fellowship" in the New Testament [Greek *koinōnia*]), eating meals together,[1] and worshiping according to the liturgy of the synagogue[2] with added material focusing on the worship of Jesus.

These were strange and difficult days for new believers in Jesus in Jerusalem. The Jesus movement was viewed with suspicion and hostility. It would soon face persecution. Those involved in trade perhaps found that they were being boycotted because of their newfound faith in Jesus. No trade meant no food in their pantries. Hence the unusual (and temporary) measure of keeping "all things in common" to help those on the edge of poverty (Acts 2:44; cf. 4:32, 34–35).

In these early days, the Jesus movement was still engaged in some aspects of temple worship, but this would not last long. The sacrificial system belonged to the era of the Old Testament and was no longer necessary, and believers would soon turn away from the temple and its practices. Daily the Lord added to their number "those who were being saved" (v. 47).

Luke does not record an explicit temporal indication, and when we find Peter attending the temple at "the ninth hour" (3 p.m.; 3:1), the hour of prayer, it isn't clear how much time has passed since the events of Pentecost. What he saw that afternoon, he had probably seen many times before. Every day, a lame man was carried to the Beautiful Gate[3] and set down to beg for his food (v. 2). But today was to be a very different experience!

We learn in the next chapter that the lame man "was more than forty years old" (4:22). Perhaps he had been brought to the outer entrance of the temple since he was a teenager, and if that is indeed the case, he has been in this same spot, begging, for twenty-five years.! Everyone would have known him. Some would have thrown a shekel in his direction more than once. But today, Peter will heal him, and the event will have an enormous impact. It was not something done in a corner; rather, it was done in plain sight and in front of a large crowd of people.

As Peter passes by, the lame man calls out for "alms" (3:3). The Greek word (eleēmosynēn) implies "pity" or "mercy." Jesus, in the Sermon on the Mount, had encouraged generosity to those in need: "Give to the one who begs from you, and do not refuse the one who would borrow from you" (Matt. 5:42). The centurion Cornelius demonstrated that he was a faithful follower of the Lord by giving alms (Acts 10:1–2).

Peter, however, had no money that day to give to the lame man. As he and John caught the man's attention, Peter said: "I have no silver and gold, but what I do have I give to you. In the name of Jesus Christ of Nazareth, rise up and walk!" (3:6). When Peter pulled him up, the man was no longer lame, and he jumped for joy and entered the temple with Peter and John, leaping about as he went (vv. 7–8). The crowds saw him, and hearing the commotion, others ran to the vicinity of the portico of Solomon where the man and the Apostles to whom he clung were to be found (vv. 9–11).

This is the first recorded miracle that Peter has performed. It is a sign that he is an Apostle (2 Cor. 12:12). Miracles occur sporadically in the New Testament, and always sparingly and purposefully. There were no doubt others in Jerusalem with various ailments, but they were not healed. Had Peter and the other Apostles begun a systematic campaign of healing, it would have detracted from their main purpose: to advance the kingdom of God through the preaching of the gospel.

A crowd now gathers, and they are paying attention to Peter. It is an opportunity to preach once more. This is the second recorded sermon from Peter.

Covenant Theology

Examining the content of Peter's second sermon reveals fascinating insights into how he understood the Old Testament as *one* narrative, *one* story leading to a definite conclusion. Peter shows no tendency to view what is happening in Jerusalem after the life and death of Jesus as something of a parenthesis. It was for Peter a fulfillment and continuation of a story that begins in the first book of the Torah, Genesis.

What is the Old Testament essentially about? What is its *singular* message? In my years as a seminary professor, I was always fascinated whenever the faculty interviewed a possible new hire, particularly if that hire was for the Old Testament department. One Old Testament professor always asked the same question: "How was a person saved in the old covenant era?" The question seemed simple—too simple, I initially thought. If the candidate hesitated or prevaricated or took too long to answer the question *simply*, we all knew that he would fail the interview. The answer that the professor expected was "In precisely the same way as in the new covenant—by faith alone in the promised Savior alone." That answer demonstrates a fundamental understanding that the Old Testament is where a promise is made and that the New Testament is where we see that promise fulfilled. It understands that *one* covenant of grace operates in both administrations.

Peter begins by referring to the patriarchs, Abraham, Isaac, and Jacob, saying that their God was the One who "glorified his servant Jesus" (Acts 3:13). What had happened in Jerusalem—the arrest, trial, and crucifixion of Jesus, followed by His glorious resurrection and ascension—was part of a narrative that began with the patriarchs.

And not just the patriarchs. The prophets also spoke of Christ: "What God foretold by the mouth of all the prophets, that his Christ would suffer, he thus fulfilled" (v. 18). Just as he had done in his first Pentecost sermon, pointing out that it was a fulfillment of a prophecy by the prophet Joel, so in this second sermon Peter does the same. The Jesus whom the Jews in Jerusalem had rejected ("you killed the Author of life"; v. 15) was "the Christ appointed for [them]" (v. 20). The prophets were united on the focus of their message: "All the prophets who have spoken, from Samuel and those who came after him, also proclaimed these days" (v. 24).

And Peter is not finished pointing out the lines of continuity from the Old

Testament. He also mentions Moses' prophecy of "a prophet like [Moses]" to whom they should listen (Acts 3:22, quoting Deut. 18:15, 18–19). This passage in Deuteronomy is one of the markers for how to read the Old Testament as *one* consistent message. It is yet another advance on what was said earlier in Genesis 3:15:

> "I will put enmity between you and the woman,
>> and between your offspring and her offspring;
> he shall bruise your head,
>> and you shall bruise his heel."

The "offspring" of the woman who will destroy the works of the devil (1 John 3:8) will come in the form of a prophet like Moses. When John the Baptist gathered large crowds to hear him preach, people inquired, "Are you the Prophet?" (John 1:21). Peter answers that question. John the Baptist was not; Jesus is. And all who fail to "listen to that prophet shall be destroyed from the people" (Acts 3:23).

Tim Keller recalls the Ligonier Valley Study Center, just outside the little western Pennsylvania hamlet of Stahlstown, where R.C. Sproul was hosting his regular weekly question and answer session with a British Old Testament scholar, J. Alec Motyer. They were addressing this question of the essence of the Old Testament and its relationship to the New Testament. At one point, Motyer told the audience to imagine how an Old Testament believer might give his testimony:

> We were in a foreign land, in bondage, under the sentence of death. But our mediator—the one who stands between us and God—came to us with the promise of deliverance. We trusted in the promises of God, took shelter under the blood of the lamb, and he led us out. Now we are on the way to the Promised Land. We are not there yet, of course, but we have the law to guide us, and through blood sacrifice we also have his presence in our midst. So he will stay with us until we get to our true country, our everlasting home.

And, Motyer added, "[We] could say the same thing, almost word for word."[4]

God's Servant

Peter makes four claims concerning Jesus.

First, Jesus is God's *servant*. Second, He is the *Holy and Righteous One*. Third, Jesus is the *Author of life*. Fourth, Jesus is *glorified*.

Jesus is God's "servant" (Acts 3:13, 26). As we have already noted, Jesus viewed His own identity in terms of the Suffering Servant Songs of Isaiah (Isa. 42:1–4; 49:1–6; 50:4–11; 52:13–53:12). In response to the exuberant desire of the Sons of Thunder, James and John, to serve Jesus faithfully, Jesus responded, "For even the Son of Man came not to be served but to serve, and to give his life as a ransom for many" (Mark 10:45). The statement summarizes, almost completely, who Jesus was and what He came to do. Notably, He saw Himself as a servant and, in using the word "many," seems to be quoting the closing lines of the fourth Servant Song, "he bore the sin of *many*" (Isa. 53:12, emphasis added).

Paul also underlined this aspect of Jesus' identity in his letter to the Philippians: "Though he was in the form of God, [he] did not count equality with God a thing to be grasped, but emptied himself, by taking the form of a servant, being born in the likeness of men. And being found in human form, he humbled himself by becoming obedient to the point of death, even death on a cross" (Phil. 2:6–8). Jesus took the form of a servant. He came to serve by giving His life as a substitute for sinners, thereby appeasing the wrath of God.

Second, Jesus is "the Holy and Righteous One" (Acts 3:14). Seven times, God is referred to as "the Holy One" in Isaiah (Isa. 29:23; 30:15; 43:3; 48:17; 54:5; 55:5; 60:9). And in the fourth Servant Song, the servant is called "the righteous one" (53:11).

Jesus is without sin. He stands apart from the rest of humanity. He is the law keeper and covenant keeper. He stands in our place, providing the obedience that we cannot: "For our sake he made him to be sin who knew no sin, so that in him we might become the righteousness of God" (2 Cor. 5:21). More especially, decades later, Peter would still insist on the righteousness of Christ: "For Christ also suffered once for sins, the righteous for the unrighteous, that he might bring us to God, being put to death in the flesh but made alive in the spirit" (1 Peter 3:18).

There was no other good enough
    to pay the price of sin;
he only could unlock the gate
    of heav'n, and let us in.[5]

Third, Jesus is "the Author of life" (Acts 3:15). In addition to Peter's designation, the writer of Hebrews referred to Jesus as the Author of salvation (Heb. 2:10), as well as the Author and Finisher of our faith (12:2). The Greek word for "Author" (*archēgon*) can also be rendered "pioneer" or "trailblazer."[6] It suggests someone whose achievements make it possible for others to follow in that person's footsteps.

Jesus had made it possible for Peter to experience life in its fullness, with purpose and clarity. Peter knew the purpose of his existence. Peter had been "born again to a living hope through the resurrection of Jesus Christ from the dead" (1 Peter 1:3). He was writing to fellow believers who had experienced the same thing: "You have been born again, not of perishable seed but of imperishable, through the living and abiding word of God" (v. 23). "I came that they may have life and have it abundantly," Jesus said (John 10:10).

Fourth, Jesus is "glorified" (Acts 3:13). God "raised [him] from the dead" and set Him in a place of glory (v. 15; cf. v. 26). The Father has put Jesus' true identity on full display. He sits at the right hand of God in majestic splendor. And this is something that all believers can look forward to. We will share in the glory one day. "So is it with the resurrection of the dead. What is sown is perishable; what is raised is imperishable. It is sown in dishonor; it is raised in glory. It is sown in weakness; it is raised in power. It is sown a natural body; it is raised a spiritual body. If there is a natural body, there is also a spiritual body" (1 Cor. 15:42–44). Peter was preaching that day something that he would express again in his first epistle. He was preaching about "the sufferings of Christ and the subsequent glories" (1 Peter 1:11). Jesus must remain in that glory "until the time for restoring all the things about which God spoke by the mouth of his holy prophets long ago" (Acts 3:21).

Repentance

There was something that Peter's listeners needed to do in response to this word about Christ. There always is.

And what is that? *Repent!*

Peter speaks about the people of Jerusalem's having acted in "ignorance" (Acts 3:17). What does he mean? Is he absolving them of any guilt in the matter of Jesus' crucifixion? Certainly not. In his first and second sermons, he had been blunt in placing the blame for Jesus' death *on them* (2:23; 3:15). Some had been complicit in the death of Jesus. And some had gone along with the mob, unsure of what was going on. They, too, were culpable. And yet there were degrees of culpability. For some, it was an act that they went along with in ignorance, as compared with those who were the ringleaders of the plot that killed Jesus.

But now, in the light of all that they have heard about who Jesus is and what He has done on behalf of sinners, it is time to repent. They must turn away from their sins and turn to Jesus. They must ask forgiveness and know that they will receive it if they are sincere (cf. Acts 3:26). And if they do repent, what can they expect? Their sins will be "blotted out" (v. 19). The Greek (*exaleiphthēai*) suggests a washing. Their filthy stains will be removed.

They can also expect "times of refreshing" (v. 20). The Greek (*anapsyxeōs*) suggests that their souls, their innermost selves, will be restored. Something new has happened, and they can experience it for themselves.

Peter always seems to be thinking about the glory. They can expect to be a part of the final state, "the time for restoring all the things" (v. 21). The Greek (*apokatastaseōs*) is the same word that the disciples used in Acts 1:6 when they had mistakenly thought that this event was about to take place there and then. It wasn't. But one day it will come to pass, and believers will share in it.

Finish, then, thy new creation;
pure and spotless let us be:
let us see thy great salvation
perfectly restored in thee;
changed from glory into glory,
'til in heav'n we take our place,
'til we cast our crowns before thee,
lost in wonder, love, and praise.[7]

14

Prison Time

"I turn back to the years of my imprisonment and say, sometimes to the astonishment of those about me, 'Bless you, prison.' I have served enough time there. I nourished my soul there, and I say without hesitation: 'Bless you, prison, for having been in my life.'"[1]

So wrote Alexander Solzhenitsyn, the Russian novelist and dissident, after being imprisoned by Joseph Stalin in the 1940s.

Imprisonment can change your life. And for Peter, it emboldened him.

Peter and John's preaching in the temple area annoyed the temple hierarchy, particularly the Sadducees (Acts 4:1–2). The Sadducees were a sociopolitical sect of Judaism that rose to significant power during the Second Temple era. Their responsibilities lay in the maintenance of temple matters. In particular, they did not believe in the immortality of the soul or the resurrection of the body. Peter's preaching placed the resurrection of Jesus front and center (vv. 2, 10).

The Sadducees' intervention was brought about by the healing of the lame man (3:6–10; 4:22). But more especially, it was the bold preaching of Jesus' resurrection that got Peter and John into trouble: "The Sadducees came upon them, greatly annoyed because they were teaching the people and proclaiming in Jesus the resurrection from the dead" (4.1–2).

Peter and John were arrested and put in custody, probably somewhere in the temple area where Jewish temple police kept order (see v. 1, "the captain of the temple"). Luke, in retelling the incident, wants us to know that when bad things happen, there is also a narrative of providence and blessing. Bad things may occur to one person to be a blessing to another. Think of the story of Joseph. Peter and John's imprisonment made many Jews think about what Peter and John had been saying, and many of those Jews believed it. Luke tells us that "many of those who had heard the word believed, and the number of the men came to about five thousand" (v. 4). This is probably not in addition to the three thousand mentioned earlier at Pentecost (2:41). The population of Jerusalem in the first century is estimated to be more than half a million. Five thousand represents less than 1 percent, but it is a measure of just how much of a threat this Jesus movement was to the stability of the temple administration that the Sadducean hierarchy orders the arrest and overnight imprisonment of Peter and John. The number now following Jesus may be small, but it had every potential of growing, and for the Sadducees, it needed to be stopped.

Filled with the Holy Spirit

It was evening when Peter and John were arrested, and the next day, the full temple hierarchy gathered, including rulers, elders, scribes, and the high-priestly family, among whom were Annas and Caiaphas, who had been central in the trial of Jesus. They might have thought that Jesus' crucifixion would be the end of the Jesus movement, but they were greatly mistaken. The movement was growing, and it was time to nip it in the bud, once and for all, lest the entire city be affected.

The central question put to Peter and John the next morning was in relation to the healing of the lame man the previous day: "By what power or by what name did you do this?" (Acts 4:7). The fact of his healing was not in dispute. But how exactly had it come about? What trickery or magic was at play? Worse, was this some demonic power? Rather than be awed by the healing, the rulers see it as a threat to the stability of the temple administration and to their own governance. Peter's actions had threatened the stability of temple administration.

Luke tells us that the secret to Peter's powers of healing and effective preaching was the Holy Spirit. Peter was *"filled* with the Holy Spirit" (v. 8, emphasis added; cf. v. 31). This is the second time that Luke has drawn attention to the Holy Spirit's *filling* the Apostles and believers in Jerusalem (cf. 2:4). And it will not be the last (9:17; 13:9, 52).

Having been filled by the Holy Spirit at Pentecost, Peter, as Luke indicates, *continues* to be filled by the Spirit, who emboldens him in a moment of trial to stand firm and not to buckle as he had done during Jesus' trial.

Every Christian is indwelled by the Holy Spirit. Believers do not have a part of the Spirit; they have *Him*. The Spirit makes His home within the heart of every Christian and dwells there (Rom. 8:9). The Spirit creates a new heart, enabling sinners to repent and believe in the Lord Jesus. In that sense, every Christian is *filled* with the Holy Spirit. But Paul also adds the exhortation to "*be filled* with the Spirit" (Eph. 5:18, emphasis added), making it our responsibility that we always call upon the Spirit to aid us in our pilgrimage.

Luke is telling us in his account of Peter's arrest and imprisonment that a special ministry of the Holy Spirit, over and above His normal work of indwelling, was given to Peter to animate him to be courageous and faithful when facing his accusers. These men standing before him had power to ensure that Peter would never be heard again. They had shown their malice in their insistence that Jesus be put to death. And they could do the same now with the Apostles and deal with this potential threat once and for all. Peter needs the fullness of the Holy Spirit more than ever right now.

The Holy Spirit continues to engage in this ministry of strengthening and empowering in the lives of believers today. When courage is needed, we are to call on Him to fill us anew and encourage us to be faithful and true to our Savior.

By the Name of Jesus Christ

Peter's response to the question put to him by the temple authorities is a lesson in courage and loyalty. He doesn't flinch or dilute his answer: "Let it be known to all of you and to all the people of Israel that by the name of Jesus Christ of Nazareth, whom you crucified, whom God raised from the dead—by him this man is standing before you well" (Acts 4:10).

Peter was asked the source of the power or the *name* by which the healing had occurred. His response was to say that it was in "the name of Jesus Christ of Nazareth." The One that these authorities had killed was raised from the dead and is alive and working in their midst by His representative agent, the Holy Spirit.

Once again, Peter reveals his knowledge of the Old Testament, especially those passages that spoke of the coming of Christ. These were passages that he had carefully studied while listening to Jesus for three years. They had formed the contours of how he understood the message of the Old Testament as a whole, as a grand narrative of the coming Messiah, who would deliver His people from bondage.

Peter's response mimics the sermons that we have already heard him preach. His message doesn't change. He makes no attempt to downplay or soften his answer to secure his release. He could have easily reasoned that to moderate his response at this moment might be the better part of valor. There would be another day when he could be bold. But Peter, the "rock," showed his mettle, exhibiting a strength that came from the ministry of the Holy Spirit within him.

Peter must have always been fascinated by stones and rocks, particularly cornerstones of significant buildings. After all, Jesus had addressed him as a rock at Caesarea Philippi. Psalm 118, the last of the Hallel psalms read at Passover, drew his attention:

> The stone that the builders rejected
>> has become the cornerstone.
> This is the LORD's doing;
>> it is marvelous in our eyes. (Ps. 118:22–23, quoted in Acts 4:11)

The "stone" in view in this psalm was Jesus. And the psalm became something of an obsession for Peter. He quotes it again in his first epistle (1 Peter 2:7).

Watching how Peter reads the Old Testament will help us find the highway that takes us from Genesis to Malachi and into the New Testament. It is the Jesus highway, and finding it provides a sure path to guide us as we read God's Word.

Resurrection and Exclusivity

It has become clear that the message of the resurrection was central to the good news preached by the Apostles. God raised Jesus from the dead (Acts 4:10). It is not simply the *fact* of Jesus' resurrection; it is the *meaning* and *implication* of it. As we have seen, the resurrection of Christ is at the heart of the good news (2:24, 31–32; 3:15, 22, 26; 4:2, 10, 33).

Christianity rises or falls on the certainty of the historical resurrection of Christ. Without the empty tomb, there is no good news, and Christianity descends into moralism. For Peter, as well as for Paul, the resurrection was indisputable proof that Jesus was both Savior and Lord (Acts 1:3; 2:24–35; 3:15; 4:10; 5:30–32; 13:33–37). The resurrection shows Jesus' victory over death (2:24; 1 Cor. 15:54–57). It vindicated Jesus as righteous—you cannot keep a good man down (John 16:10). It "declared [him] to be the Son of God in power" (Rom. 1:4), and it led to His enthronement and reign at God's right hand (Phil. 2:9–11). Peter had seen Jesus several times after His resurrection, and he wasn't going to keep quiet about it.

The resurrection set Jesus apart from all other claimants to deity. It emboldened Peter to declare that "there is salvation in no one else, for there is no other name under heaven given among men by which we must be saved" (Acts 4:12).

It has become fashionable to suggest that men and women who have never heard of Jesus can be saved. Books have recently emerged with attractive titles, such as *Love Wins*[2] and *A Generous Orthodoxy*,[3] suggesting a "wider" hope and an "anonymous Christianity."[4] But Jesus Himself made it very clear that apart from faith in Him, no one is saved: "I am the way, and the truth, and the life. No one comes to the Father except through me" (John 14:6).

The exclusivity of Jesus as the way of salvation shaped the direction of the early church. At first, Christianity took shelter beneath the favored relationship that Rome displayed toward Judaism, but this insistence on Jesus' exclusivity would rip Christianity away and place it in the spotlight of Rome's ire. If Jesus *alone* is the only way to eternal life, Rome's pantheon of gods are mere idols. Their religion is bogus and blasphemous. Peter's courage, therefore, is on display. His words will have consequences.

Boldness

Peter's "boldness" (Greek *parrēsia*) was apparent to his accusers (Acts 4:13; cf. v. 29). And what shocked them more was his knowledge, given that they regarded him as "uneducated" and "common" (v. 13). This is a typical assessment of urban dwellers about "country folk." All the disciples were Galilean, and Peter was no more than a fisherman. Peter did not have the profound schooling in philosophy and the arts that folk in Jerusalem might have had. Still, he knew his Old Testament, and he had been schooled for three years by Jesus. What better education could one wish for? Jesus had taught Peter how to read his Bible and how to understand it. And such knowledge had made him bold.

"Boldness" is a term that Luke uses eleven times in Acts. It begins and ends his narrative (4:13, 29, 31; 9:27–28; 13:46; 14:3; 18:26; 19:8; 26:26; 28:31). It is something for which Peter and the other believers pray for once this inquisition is done (4:29). It is something that we, too, should pray for. As Peter later wrote, we must be prepared "to make a defense to anyone who asks [us] for a reason for the hope that is in [us]" (1 Peter 3:15).

Having conferred with one another, Peter's accusers charged Peter and the others not to speak further in the name of Jesus (Acts 4:16–17). It was an impossible demand on men filled with the Holy Spirit, empowered to speak of Jesus to all who would listen. And Peter and John's response is immediate and resolute: "Whether it is right in the sight of God to listen to you rather than to God, you must judge, for we cannot but speak of what we have seen and heard" (vv. 19–20).

In general, we are to obey legal authorities. Peter wrote as much in his first epistle: "Be subject for the Lord's sake to every human institution, whether it be to the emperor as supreme, or to governors as sent by him to punish those who do evil and to praise those who do good. For this is the will of God, that by doing good you should put to silence the ignorance of foolish people" (1 Peter 2:13–15). We are to render to Caesar what is Caesar's (Mark 12:17). But this is not an *absolute* command, without exception. When Caesar asks what God forbids, we must obey God rather than Caesar and take whatever consequences follow such disobedience. Peter the Coward has disappeared. Peter the Bold has emerged.

15

The Limits
of Obedience

Peter made it clear to the temple authorities that there are limits to obedience. When human authorities demand what God forbids, there can
be no ambiguity. God must be obeyed above all else. Having told the temple
heavyweights that he could do no other than speak about Jesus, Peter, along
with John, was released from prison (Acts 4:19–22).

There followed a time of prayer during which the believers, the Apostles, and others prayed specifically for *boldness*. The second psalm drove their
understanding of what had occurred. The rage of human authorities was not
directed, first of all, against the Apostles and their preaching; it was instead
set against the Lord and "his Anointed" (Acts 4:26, quoting Ps. 2:1–2). What
had happened in Jerusalem was a fulfillment of what redemptive history had
witnessed from the very beginning: the powers of darkness were attempting
to destroy God's plan to save sinners. But God has control of this narrative.
The enemies' plans are but the outworking of a greater causality: Pilate and
the temple leaders were doing "whatever [God's] hand and [God's] plan . . .
predestined to take place" (Acts 4:28). And knowing this certainty of divine
sovereignty, the believers, the Apostles, and others prayed for boldness (v. 29).

The place where they gathered shook, and they were once again filled
with the Holy Spirit (v. 31). John Chrysostom, in the great city of Constantinople, began to preach what turned out to be a series of fifty-five sermons
on Acts. In his eleventh homily, on Acts 4:23, he notes, "The whole place was
shaken and that left them all the more unshaken."[1]

We next meet Peter in Acts 5, after the tragic and shocking deaths of Ananias and Sapphira. Sometime later, Peter and the other Apostles gathered in Solomon's Portico, the part of the temple where Peter, John, and the healed lame man had gathered (v. 12; cf. 3:11). Though Peter was held in high esteem, the other believers kept their distance from him. The last time that Peter and John were in Solomon's Portico, they had been arrested and put into prison overnight.

It appears that after their release from prison, Peter and the other Apostles engaged in healing miracles and "signs and wonders" (5:12). People came from far and wide, laying the sick on "cots and mats" in the street so that Peter's shadow might be cast on them (v. 15). "And they were all healed" (v. 16).

It is hard to understand the mentality of the high priest and the Sadducees. Instead of showing gratitude for these extraordinary healings, they are filled with "jealousy" (v. 17). Peter and the other Apostles were again arrested and put into prison (v. 18). Luke describes the place of their incarceration as the "public prison" (v. 18), suggesting a different location from the one we heard about in Acts 4.[2]

The followers of Jesus were a threat to the stability of Jerusalem. And the Apostles were the cause of it. The Jewish leaders needed to shut them up for a while. Little did they, or for that matter the Apostles, know what would happen that first night. "An angel of the Lord opened the prison doors and brought them out" (5:19). A spectacular angelic jailbreak!

Life

Peter might have wondered where the angel was taking him. Was he being escorted to a safe house, somewhere outside the city? No, he was told to return to the temple and start preaching again "all the words of this Life" (Acts 5:20).

First, it is somewhat unexpected that they would be asked to return to the scene of the crime. Was there to be no period of silence and rest to ward off Jewish anger at their behavior? Apparently not. Peter and John were to return to the temple, wait perhaps for Jews to arrive for early-morning prayers at "daybreak," and start preaching the good news (v. 21).

Second, the angel describes the message that they will proclaim as "all the words of this Life" (v. 20). Earlier, Peter referred to Jesus as "the Author of life" (3:15). The ESV capitalizes "Life" in Acts 5:20, suggesting that what the angel has in mind is not only a message that says "Jesus will give life, true and everlasting life" but also a message that centers on Jesus as the *source* and *embodiment* of life.

Evidently, a storm was brewing among the temple leaders. Early in the morning, the high priest and his entourage called for a meeting of the senate, the seventy-one-member Sanhedrin, or supreme court (v. 21). The Greek word for "senate" is *gerousia*, from the word *geron*, the Greek word for "old." The Sanhedrin was made up of old men, but their chief problem wasn't age; it was unbelief.

Officers were sent to the prison to bring Peter and John before them, but when the officers returned, they told the high priest that they had found the prison doors locked and the guards standing outside, but when they opened the doors, no one was inside (vv. 21–23). To their great surprise, someone came and told them that the men they had arrested were in the temple and were teaching the people gathering for morning prayer (v. 25). The captain of the temple went and brought the Apostles into the court, but "not by force, for they were afraid of being stoned by the people" (v. 26). Apparently, daily life in the temple could easily become stormy, since the chief of security was afraid of being stoned.

Peter was questioned by the high priest, *not* about the manner of his jailbreak but about what he had been doing in the temple that morning. The high priest was hardly likely to believe the story that Peter would relate about an angelic visitation.

To Obey or Not to Obey

Peter had been told not to preach in the name of Jesus, but he went and did it anyway. It was a command that he found impossible to obey. The high priest was most concerned about the rising number of Jesus-followers and sympathizers and that the Apostles were acting in a manner designed "to bring this man's blood upon us" (Acts 5:28). The high priest and Saducean followers had blood on their hands. They had been complicit in the death of Jesus. And they knew it.

Peter answered the high priest's question by insisting, "We must obey God rather than men" (v. 29). As we saw in the previous chapter, there are limits to obedience. There are occasions when obeying earthly power is morally wrong.

Think of the Hebrew midwives in Exodus 1 who disobeyed the pharaoh's orders to kill the male children. Or Daniel, refusing the edict not to pray in public except in the name of King Darius. Or Esther, coming directly before the king to plead on behalf of the Jews, something that was forbidden. All these are righteous violations of the authority of the state. They were instances when the state asked of believers something that they could not do in good conscience. When Peter, or Paul, commands obedience to earthly powers, he does so with this principle in mind: Obey so long as, in doing so, you are not violating something that God requires. It is never right to obey the state when God's commands are being violated in the process (see Rom. 13:1–7; 1 Peter 2:18–19).

In responding to the high priest, Peter (and Luke in recording it) gives a summary of the gospel in two verses: "The God of our fathers raised Jesus, whom you killed by hanging him on a tree. God exalted him at his right hand as Leader and Savior, to give repentance to Israel and forgiveness of sins" (Acts 5:30–31).

I once preached a series of about a dozen sermons on the theme "What Is the Gospel?" At the end of the series, the professor in me made me ask the congregation to send me their answer to the question in less than a hundred words. The responses—and there were many—were fascinating and encouraging. These thirty-six words (in English) of Peter's would be a perfect answer.

Notice the emphasis on Jesus. There is not only an emphasis on Jesus' *person*; there is also a stress on His death and resurrection. Both Peter and the Holy Spirit are witnesses to both events of that momentous weekend (Acts 5:32). Peter's message is about *Jesus*: who He is and what He has done for us. It is almost an obsession:

- "Men of Israel, hear these words: Jesus of Nazareth, a man attested to you by God with mighty works and wonders and signs that God did through him in your midst, as you yourselves know—this Jesus, delivered up according to the definite plan and foreknowledge of God, you crucified and killed by the hands of lawless men." (2:22–23)
- "I have no silver and gold, but what I do have I give to you. In the name of Jesus Christ of Nazareth, rise up and walk!" (3:6)

- "The God of Abraham, the God of Isaac, and the God of Jacob, the God of our fathers, glorified his servant Jesus, whom you delivered over and denied in the presence of Pilate, when he had decided to release him. But you denied the Holy and Righteous One, and asked for a murderer to be granted to you, and you killed the Author of life, whom God raised from the dead." (3:13–15)
- "Let it be known to all of you and to all the people of Israel that by the name of Jesus Christ of Nazareth, whom you crucified, whom God raised from the dead—by him this man is standing before you well." (4:10)

C.H. Spurgeon once wrote:

You may, perhaps, have read the life of Audubon, the celebrated American naturalist. He spent the major part of his life in preparing a very valuable work on the birds of America. He tracked these birds into their remotest haunts, painted them from nature, lived in the cane-brakes, swamps, and prairies—even among the red men, exposed to all kinds of dangers—and all simply to become a complete ornithologist. When he was in Paris, collecting subscriptions for his new work, his diary was full of wretchedness—there was nothing in Paris for him and the only bright dream that he had was when he saw the stock-pigeons building their nests in the garden of the Tuileries. The broad streets, the magnificent palaces, the pictures of the Louvre, these were all nothing to him—the stock-pigeons everything. He came to London, and he was equally dull there. Not a single incident shows a comfortable frame of mind, till he sees one day a flock of wild geese passing over the city. He wrote in London a paper on birds; and he says "While I am writing I think I hear the rustle of the wings of pigeons in the backwoods of America." The man's soul was full of birds, nothing but birds; and of course he became a great naturalist. He lived and he was willing to die for birds. We need to muster a band of ministers who live only for Christ, and desire nothing but opportunities for promoting His glory—opportunities for spreading His truth—opportunities for winning by power those whom Jesus has redeemed by His precious blood. Men of one idea—these are they that shall do exploits in the camp of Israel.[3]

Having spoken, the members of the Sanhedrin are furious, and they want to kill Peter and the other Apostles. The Apostles have a price on their heads (Acts 5:33). Had it not been for the intervention of Gamaliel, the noted rabbi who taught Saul of Tarsus (was the young Saul in the city at this time?), the Sanhedrin's fury might have been unleashed on the Apostles.

Instead, they beat Peter and the other Apostles, charging them once more not to speak in the name of Jesus, before letting them go (v. 40).

Luke adds a description of Peter's response: "Then they left the presence of the council, rejoicing that they were counted worthy to suffer dishonor for the name" (v. 41). Peter reflected the same disposition in his first epistle: "Beloved, do not be surprised at the fiery trial when it comes upon you to test you, as though something strange were happening to you. But rejoice insofar as you share Christ's sufferings, that you may also rejoice and be glad when his glory is revealed. If you are insulted for the name of Christ, you are blessed, because the Spirit of glory and of God rests upon you" (1 Peter 4:12–14).

Did Peter obey the chief priest? Of course not! He and his brothers went daily to the temple and proclaimed the gospel of Jesus Christ (Acts 5:42).

A gospel lion, filled with the Holy Spirit, has been unleashed.

16

Crab Is
on the Menu

By now, Saul of Tarsus has entered the story. He had his hand in the stoning of Stephen. Luke tells us that he "approved of [Stephen's] execution" (Acts 8:1). The event was brutal, and it unleashed a torrent of persecution against the church in Jerusalem, scattering young believers into Judea and Samaria. The Apostles, however, remained in the city, prepared to meet whatever harassment came their way. Saul entered "house after house" and, by discovering Christian symbols or simply asking whether the residents were followers of Jesus, had those who remained in the city summarily arrested and taken to prison (v. 3). Saul was on a mission to eradicate the heresy of the Jesus movement once and for all. And he came within an inch of succeeding.

But then the unthinkable occurred: Saul of Tarsus was converted! Hot with anger against these Jesus-followers, he had gone to the high priest to ask for official letters that he might use to arrest those belonging "to the Way" (9:2; cf. 19:9, 23; 22:4; 24:14, 22). He was heading for the synagogues of Damascus, presumably the first of many cities that Saul intended to visit. On the road to Damascus, he was surrounded by a light from heaven. And then he heard a voice: "Saul, Saul, why are you persecuting me?" (9:4). Asking for the identity of the voice, he was told, "I am Jesus" (v. 5).

Had Saul been in Jerusalem when Jesus was crucified? Perhaps. Had he stood among the crowds watching the soldiers nail Him to a cross? Perhaps. Had he heard that claims were made that Jesus had risen from the dead?

Absolutely. But he had not believed them. Jesus was an enemy, and He was dead. But to Saul's absolute astonishment, Jesus was speaking to him.

How could this be? Blinded by the experience, Saul was taken by his companions to Damascus to recover at the house of Judas on Straight Street (9:7–11). A disciple named Ananias was divinely instructed to go to Saul to heal his sight. Reluctantly, Ananias agreed, staggering from the message he heard from the Lord regarding Saul: "Go, for he is a chosen instrument of mine to carry my name before the Gentiles and kings and the children of Israel. For I will show him how much he must suffer for the sake of my name" (vv. 15–16).

And so it happened. Saul's sight was restored. He was told that Jesus, whom he had encountered on the road to Damascus, had sent Ananias to him with a message. Saul was now a follower of Jesus. And he was baptized (v. 18). His life would never be the same again. He immediately began to preach in synagogues in Damascus and then went to Arabia for a season before returning to Damascus (cf. Gal. 1:17). Some identify Arabia as modern-day Jordan, but others think that Saul went to Mount Sinai because he identifies Mount Sinai as being in Arabia (Gal. 4:25). His exit from Damascus was dramatic. The Jews wanted to kill him, viewing him now as a traitor. To prevent Saul's being killed, he was lowered from the walls of the city in a basket, to make his exit to Arabia (Acts 9:24–25).

At some point, Saul made his way to Jerusalem, where he was introduced to the disciples in the city, who were understandably skittish about his new-found faith in Jesus (v. 26). Was it a plot? Was Saul a spy, attempting to gain more information about the leadership of the followers of Jesus?

It was Barnabas who persuaded the disciples as to Saul's genuine conversion (v. 27). They listened to Saul preach boldly in the name of the Lord and were convinced. Others were convinced, too, and were ready to kill him. These were the "Hellenists" to whom Saul preached (v. 29). Probably former associates of Saul who had helped mount the attack on Stephen, they were now incensed that their former ally was a traitor. It is all too clear that Saul would not last very long, given that "they were seeking to kill him" (v. 29). His friends, therefore, took him down to Caesarea and put him on a ship that would take him to Tarsus (v. 30), "the regions of Syria and Cilicia" (Gal. 1:21).

For now, Saul is out of the picture, and Peter remains the top Apostle.

Lydda, Joppa, and Caesarea

At Joppa (today's Jaffa, part of Tel Aviv), on the Mediterranean coast, a woman by the Aramaic name of Tabitha[1] became ill and subsequently died (Acts 9:36–37). Peter, who was about ten miles inland at a place called Lydda, had healed a man called Aeneas, who had been bedridden for eight years (vv. 32–35). As a result, many had come to faith in Christ.

Hearing that Peter was nearby, two disciples were sent to bring Peter to Joppa. Upon his arrival, Peter was taken to an upper room where women were crying and displaying garments that Tabitha had made for them. Perhaps to gather his senses, he ejected the women, knelt beside Tabitha's corpse, and prayed. Turning to the body, Peter said, "Tabitha, arise" (v. 40). "And he gave her his hand and raised her up. Then, calling the saints and widows, he presented her alive" (v. 41).

It made quite the stir. People talked about this miracle, and many came to faith in Jesus. Peter stayed on in the city, lodging with Simon, a tanner (vv. 42–43). In Jewish law, tanning was an unclean profession, since it dealt with dead animals. Peter was violating his Jewish lineage in staying there. But unbeknownst to Peter, things were about to change. What he had believed his entire life regarding certain foods was going to be undone. The kosher laws would be abolished. What Peter had once considered unclean (fraternizing with gentiles, for example) would be eradicated.

Peter (and Jesus, too) had never eaten crab cakes or lobster bisque. He had strictly followed the dietary laws of Israel as spelled out in Leviticus 11 and Deuteronomy 14. To underline Israel's distinctiveness from the surrounding nations, God allowed the Jews to eat only that which chews the cud and has a split hoof. Forbidden were camels, rock badgers, hares, and, perhaps most distressingly, pigs. Peter had never tasted bacon!

Luke narrates how Peter came to know that bacon was on the menu by employing a split-screen method. First, we are introduced to a centurion named Cornelius who lived in Caesarea, some thirty miles north of Joppa and also on the Mediterranean coast.

Cornelius is Italian, a career military man having charge of 80 to 160 men. But he was also "a devout man who feared God with all his household" (Acts 10:2). He was a proselyte Jew, worshiped at the synagogue, "gave alms generously to the people, and prayed continually to God" (v. 2). One afternoon at

3, Cornelius saw a vision. An angel came to him and spoke his name and told him that his prayers had been heard. Perhaps he had focused his prayers on the need for salvation. Perhaps he had asked for someone to help him understand the gospel. He was to send for a man called Peter, who was at the house of Simon the tanner in Joppa. Two servants and a devout soldier were sent southward to fetch Peter.

Meanwhile, as the three were making their journey to Joppa, Peter was engaging in his midday prayers. He became hungry and asked for something to eat. As the food was being prepared, he fell into a trance and saw the heavens opened, with "something like a great sheet descending, being let down by its four corners upon the earth" (v. 11). Inside the sheet were animals, reptiles, and birds (v. 12). Then came a voice that said, "Rise, Peter; kill and eat" (v. 13). But it was a command that Peter could not possibly agree to because these animals that he saw were *unclean*. They were among the forbidden proteins of kosher laws.

His instinct was a good one, and his obedience was an act of piety. But it was God who was making this command. Peter had tried to correct Jesus more than once, only to find himself on the wrong side of virtue. "What God has made clean, do not call common" (v. 15), Peter was told. As though to remind him of his past sins, the vision occurred three times.

Just as Peter was pondering the meaning of the vision, the three men from Cornelius' house arrived, something that Peter heard the Spirit inform him of: "Behold, three men are looking for you" (v. 19). When Peter and the three men met, Peter was told the reason that the three were there. Cornelius, their master, needed Peter to come to him. It was now far too late in the day to make the journey to Caesarea, so the men spent the night at the house of Simon the tanner and made the journey northward the next day.

When Peter arrived in Caesarea, Cornelius was so overcome by Peter's presence, thinking that Peter might be an angel, that he got down on his knees before him, only to have Peter lift him up and say, "Stand up; I too am a man" (v. 26). If Cornelius sounds nervous, Peter's response sounds awkward. True, Peter shows some humility in not wishing to be worshiped by Cornelius. But what he says next is telling. He reminds Cornelius that as a Jew, he really shouldn't be hanging out with gentile foreigners. Yet he has come to Cornelius' house because God told him so: "God has shown me that I should not call any person common or unclean" (v. 28). Peter's understanding of the world is changing.

It is interesting that he refers to himself as a "Jew" (v. 28). Believers in Jesus did not yet think of themselves as following a separate religion. Nor were they ever to refer to themselves as "Christians." That was meant as a slur that arose later, in Antioch (11:26).

God Shows No Partiality

Peter preached a sermon in the presence of Cornelius and others that Luke condenses into ten verses (Acts 10:34–43). It begins with an observation that Peter makes based on the vision he had seen in Joppa. The vision had been about food: that no distinction ought now to be made between one animal and another. The kosher laws had played their part in the infancy of the church, but those days are gone. Jesus has come, and the Spirit has been poured out. Peter may now have pork for dinner.

But there was more to this vision than food. There was in this vision a far greater lesson about who may truly worship God. God was no longer separating Jew and gentile: "God shows no partiality" (v. 34). "There is neither Jew nor Greek, there is neither slave nor free, there is no male and female, for you are all one in Christ Jesus" (Gal. 3:28). The door into God's presence had not been altogether closed to gentiles in the Old Testament era. But "the dividing wall of hostility" has now been broken down (Eph. 2:14).

The gospel is for everybody: "In every nation anyone who fears him and does what is right is acceptable to him" (Acts 10:35). We are to "make disciples of all nations," Jesus commanded (Matt. 28:19).

What followed was familiar territory for Peter, but not for Cornelius. It was a message about "good news" and "peace through Jesus Christ," who is "Lord of all" (Acts 10:36). Peter tells the story of Jesus' baptism, His anointing by the Holy Spirit, His healing ministry, and His crucifixion, "hanging him on a tree" (v. 39). But God raised Him up again, after which Jesus showed Himself, not to all but to His disciples, who, as Peter relates, "ate and drank with him" (v. 41). And this same Jesus "commanded us to preach to the people and to testify that he is the one appointed by God to be judge of the living and the dead" (v. 42). Jesus is the One whom the Old Testament pointed to, and "everyone who believes in him receives forgiveness of sins through his name" (v. 43).

Great success followed as the Holy Spirit fell on all who heard Peter's preaching. Jewish believers who came with Peter were amazed as "the Holy Spirit was poured out even on the Gentiles" (v. 45). Scores of baptisms were witnessed in Caesarea. Peter was experiencing something like another Pentecost. The gospel, which had largely been confined to one ethnic group and one geographic locality, is now spreading across the world. And the person responsible for it, humanly speaking, is Peter. Using the keys of the kingdom, Peter is unlocking the gates and ushering gentiles into the kingdom of God.

Let ev'ry kindred, ev'ry tribe,
    on this terrestrial ball,
to him all majesty ascribe,
    and crown him Lord of all;
to him all majesty ascribe,
    and crown him Lord of all.

O that with yonder sacred throng
    we at his feet may fall;
we'll join the everlasting song,
    and crown him Lord of all;
we'll join the everlasting song,
    and crown him Lord of all.[2]

17

Basic Christianity

News of large numbers of gentiles' coming to faith in Christ and receiving the Spirit was bound to cause concern among conservative Jews in Jerusalem, even those Jews who had themselves come to regard Jesus as the long-awaited Messiah.

All manner of questions arose: Should gentile believers be circumcised? What about the food laws? It was all very well for Peter to talk about having been given a vision to say that no protein was to be considered unclean, but conservative believers in Jerusalem were not likely to be so easily convinced. And what about Shabbat, the Sabbath—should it be observed? And what about temple worship with all its rituals and holy days? If what Peter was doing was legitimate, it threatened the very fabric of Judaism. Peter needed to give an account of himself and relate what his plan might be.

When Peter went from Caesarea to Jerusalem, he found himself at the center of a significant controversy. In particular, "the circumcision party" was deeply critical of his recent actions (Acts 11:2). These were technically Jewish Christians who believed that circumcision remained a sign and seal of the covenant, even for gentiles. Among them seems to have been James, the Lord's brother.

Several years have passed since Jesus' ascension. Given that Saul of Tarsus has been converted and has subsequently spent three years in Arabia (Gal. 1:17), seven years or so may now have passed. And up until recently, the church has been largely Jewish and proselyte. True, Philip evangelized in Samaria, a ministry that Peter and John validated (Acts 8:26–40). But believers, especially in Jerusalem, were still practicing Jewish ceremonies. They viewed Jesus as the Messiah and their faith as a natural extension of Judaism.

The two major parties in the city were the Pharisees and the Sadducees. The latter did not believe in a resurrection and had nothing whatsoever to do with Jesus. The "circumcision party" was, most likely, made up of Pharisees who had come to believe in Jesus. They brought with them a strict adherence to Mosaic law and human traditions added to it over the years. In particular, the rite of circumcision was a nonnegotiable requirement for any gentile male who came to faith in Jesus. So adamant were they on the issue of circumcision that they dared to accuse Peter of malpractice. Later, they would do the same to Paul (Gal. 2:11–14; Phil. 3:2; Titus 1:10). Peter's recent activity in Caesarea and Joppa made a significant impact, and the fact that large numbers of people were professing faith in Christ but were not circumcised was a significant threat to the stability of Judaism. It was time to correct Peter and steer him in a better direction.

Luke focuses on the circumcision party's objection to Peter's recent practice of not insisting that gentile believers be circumcised. They, after all, believed in Jesus and were otherwise in Peter's corner. They began with Peter's eating habits. He "went to uncircumcised men and ate with them" (Acts 11:3). Eating with gentiles meant eating their nonkosher food. The Pharisees were upset when Jesus ate with tax collectors and sinners (Mark 2:15–17) and when Jesus' disciples didn't wash their hands before eating (7:1–5). For Jesus, food is food and cannot make one unclean. It is the heart that determines whether a person is unclean.

It wasn't so much the food that was the issue; it was the fact that Peter was engaging in fellowship with gentile Christians *without*, first of all, demanding their compliance with Jewish boundary markers such as circumcision and kosher-food laws.

I Was in Joppa, Praying

Peter relates his experience in Joppa when, at the time of midday prayer, he became hungry and asked for food. While the meal was being prepared, he found himself in a trance and saw a vision of something like a white sheet coming down from heaven containing all kinds of animals, including nonkosher ones, which he was commanded to kill and eat (Acts 11:5–7). Peter told his accusers his initial objections, how the vision was given to him three times, and then how three men arrived from Caesarea, asking him to go with them to meet Cornelius, who had also been given a vision in which he was told to send for Peter (vv. 8–14).

Peter then added: "As I began to speak, the Holy Spirit fell on them just as on us at the beginning. And I remembered the word of the Lord, how he said, 'John baptized with water, but you will be baptized with the Holy Spirit.' If then God gave the same gift to them as he gave to us when we believed in the Lord Jesus Christ, who was I that I could stand in God's way?" (vv. 15–17; cf. 10:44–48). What happened at Pentecost happened again at Caesarea. It was as though the Holy Spirit was saying to Peter (and to his listeners) that the gospel must travel across the world, even to the gentiles. The new covenant includes gentiles. The old has gone; the new has come. A new era has dawned. And with it, the ceremonial law is abolished.

Specifically, Cornelius had been told, "Peter . . . will declare to you a message by which you will be saved, you and all your household" (11:13–14). Luke is no doubt providing us with only a summary of Peter's address to the circumcision party. One imagines that the explanation took quite some time, but there is enough in the summary to help us understand the content of the "message" that Peter proclaimed to Cornelius and the gentile crowd that had gathered in Caesarea.

Jesus Is Lord

First, the message is about "the Lord Jesus Christ" (Acts 11:17). In Mark's gospel, for example, the word "Lord" (Greek *kyrios*) is used interchangeably with "God" and "Jesus" (Mark 1:3; 11:9; 12:11; cf. 7:28; 11:3). As we have already noted, it is widely believed that Mark's gospel is Peter's memoirs, and it was vital that Jesus be viewed as God. Moreover, taking but one example in Mark, when Jesus responded to the disciples' question about which commandment is the greatest, He quoted Deuteronomy 6:4, the Shema: "Hear, O Israel: The Lord our God, the Lord is one" (Mark 12:29). The Greek for "Lord" in this verse is *kyrios*, but the Hebrew of the original text in Deuteronomy is the divine name customarily pronounced these days as *Yahweh*. Jews did not pronounce the name and used the Hebrew *Adonai* in its place. And for that matter, it is highly unlikely that Peter (or Paul) pronounced the Hebrew word. What is significant is that the word *kyrios* is the equivalent of *Yahweh*. Jesus is *Yahweh*. No greater attribution could be made regarding

Jesus' identity. And it is remarkable indeed that Jews in Jerusalem had come to believe it.

There is no good news apart from the confession that Jesus is Lord. A semidivine person cannot save us. Christianity stands or falls by the true divine nature of Jesus Christ. Apart from it, we have something quite different. Those who advocate that Jesus is less than true God are betraying the very essence of Christianity, which affirms His complete deity:

> And in one Lord Jesus Christ, the only begotten Son of God, begotten of the Father before all worlds; God of God, Light of Light, very God of very God; begotten, not made, being of one substance with the Father, by whom all things were made.[1]

In the words of J. Gresham Machen, "The greatest menace to the Christian Church today comes not from the enemies outside, but from the enemies within; it comes from the presence within the Church of a type of faith and practice that is anti-Christian to the core."[2]

Second, the "message" concerns repentance. Peter cites John the Baptist, a reminder to his listeners that John's principal message had been one of repentance and offering. He came offering a baptism of repentance (Mark 1:4; Acts 19:4). The gospel contains within it a call to turn *away* from the old life of sin and turn *to* Jesus. Sinners come to Jesus empty-handed. Our repentance is necessary, but it contributes nothing to our salvation. Salvation is by grace *alone*. By nature, our lives are full of self and sin, and we need to turn around and face Jesus, who offers life and forgiveness. Leaving our sinful life behind, we embrace Him by faith and receive the life He offers. We cannot take hold of Jesus with both hands and cling to sin at the same time.

Third, the "message" concerns the ministry of the Holy Spirit. John baptized with water; Jesus baptizes with the Holy Spirit (cf. Acts 11:16). The baptism of the Spirit is not to be viewed as something the Spirit *does*; rather, it should be viewed as receiving *Him*. It is the work of the Spirit, as the representative agent of Jesus, to convict us of sin and draw us to Christ. It is by the Spirit that we repent and believe. Faith and repentance are His gifts to us. It is by the Spirit that we receive a new heart and are enabled to pursue after holiness, "without which no one will see the Lord" (Heb. 12:14). It is the work of the Holy Spirit to apply all that Christ has achieved for us in His life and death and bring us all the way home to glory.

Fourth (and we cannot avoid commenting on it), Peter viewed the gospel as a message to Cornelius "and all [his] household" (Acts 11:14). The term "household" (Greek, *oikos*) is somewhat formulaic in Acts (cf. 10:2; 16:15, 31, 34; 18:8). This is not the place to become controversial, but we should at least point out that credobaptists (who baptize believers only) and paedobaptists (who baptize the infant children of believers) differ on what to make of this word. Credobaptists point out, correctly, that nowhere does Luke specifically tell us that these households contained infants incapable of expressing faith for themselves. For credobaptists, when Luke tells us that all in the household were baptized, these would have been adult baptisms, and if young children were present, they, too, would have made a credible profession of faith.

Paedobaptists, on the other hand, see in this formulaic term something that is perfectly consonant with a continuation of a policy from the old covenant wherein the sign and seal of that covenant—circumcision—was applied to eight-day-old male infants. It is unlikely that each of these households that Luke mentions contained no infants; therefore, it is likely that baptism was applied to infants also, a sign and seal in these instances *to* faith rather than *of* faith. By the grace of God, and in God's timing, the Holy Spirit will bring these infants to saving faith, making a reality of what is promised in the sacrament of baptism. The sign and seal of the gospel is for the infants of believers too.

There is far more to the gospel than Peter tells us here in this brief account to the circumcision party, but what we have is its essence. Peter might tell you to study it and take some notes.

Obedience, for Now

Having explained himself to his detractors, Peter then appealed to their good reason: "If then God gave the same gift to them as he gave to us when we believed in the Lord Jesus Christ, who was I that I could stand in God's way?" (Acts 11:17). If God saw fit to provide a second Pentecost at Caesarea, how could Peter forbid it? His task was to obey what God had told him to do.

What God had asked of Peter was difficult. Eating pork may be one of the best things in the world to us, but it was not for Peter. People have very strong opinions about food. Vegetarians and vegans make personal life choices, and they are at liberty to do so. But these choices cannot be forced on others as a moral necessity without contradicting Scripture or the food choices that Jesus Himself made. One can only imagine that if Peter ate bacon at some point in his life, he would have realized how difficult the demands of kosher nutrition were. God did not make it easy for the Old Testament church to follow a separated life.

But as we have seen, the vision was more than just about food. It was about a way of life that included fellowship—*true* fellowship with gentile brothers and sisters. Soon the church will no longer be Jerusalem-centered, and the initial base of operations will be the church in Antioch, something that will not be easy for the leaders in Jerusalem to accept. Their world is changing, and the fledgling church in Jerusalem had better get on board quickly; the rest of the church is not going to wait for them. The Holy Spirit is moving north and west, and Jerusalem will no longer be the center of administration.

James

It is a testimony to Peter's resolute courage and obedience that he complied with God's request, going immediately to Cornelius and eating with him in his house. This may appear to be a very small thing to us, but to Peter it was contrary to the pattern of almost forty years of his life. And as we will see in the next chapter, the instinct to comply with his old life patterns will be triggered in Antioch when Paul and Peter clash in a public and memorable way. It would affect their relationship for the rest of their lives.

Present in Jerusalem as Peter defends his actions is James, Jesus' younger brother. We will hear about him in the next chapter. His position has already become important. How could it have been otherwise, since he knew Jesus better than any of them? He was able to relate stories of Jesus as a teenager and young man that none of the rest of them knew. James was a powerful presence, and some had gathered to his side, calling themselves the men "from James" (Gal. 2:12). He had evidently sided with the circumcision party. His vision was narrow and local. He needed to get "the whole world" (Matt. 24:14) into his sights, expand his horizon, and see God's cosmic purpose through the ministry of the Holy Spirit. And James' narrowness is all too prevalent in the church today. In almost every church I know, the support for world missions is the concern of a few rather than all. That should not be the case. Peter would not approve.

Peter won the day on this occasion. His detractors were silenced, convinced by his testimony, saying, "Then to the Gentiles also God has granted repentance that leads to life" (Acts 11:18). It was not going to be the end of the matter, and in the next chapter we will follow Peter's journey to Antioch, where things unravel. But for now, the church is at peace, and the Great Commission is unfolding apace.

18

The Clash
of the Titans

The movie *Clash of the Titans*[1] recounts the mythical, violent conflict between Greek gods and the humans caught in between. It is a swashbuckling tale of mythology involving two powerful forces. And in Antioch, sometime after Peter's defense of his Caesarean actions in Jerusalem, Peter finds himself in some significant disagreement with the Apostle Paul.

Peter against Paul. Somehow, and for motives that are less than virtuous, one imagines what it might have been like to have been there and watch it all unfold.

After the death of Stephen at the hands of Saul of Tarsus, a large segment of the church in Jerusalem scattered for fear of persecution. Saul was going from house to house and putting men and women into prison if they were found to be Jesus-followers (Acts 8:3). But then Saul encountered Jesus on the Damascus road and was converted. Eventually, when Barnabas came to Saul's defense, the church in Jerusalem was convinced as to his sincerity (9:27). God had done a remarkable thing: He had saved the church from its worst enemy by saving the church's worst enemy!

According to Galatians 1:18 (Luke does not relate this part of the story), upon returning from Arabia after being away for three years, Saul came to Jerusalem and spent fifteen days with Peter. The only other Apostle he saw at that time was James, the Lord's brother (v. 19). Why Peter? Because he was the "rock." To Peter Jesus gave the charge to build the church. At this point, Peter is the chief Apostle. Tensions are perhaps brewing. What role does Saul play? And what role does James play?

We have no record of what they talked about, but Peter likely related to Saul what he had heard and seen of Jesus in the three years he had spent with Him as a disciple. Peter had significant stories and information that Saul did not have.

Fourteen years later,[2] Paul[3] once again came to Jerusalem with a revelation that he had received that God intended him to be the Apostle to the gentiles, just as Peter was the Apostle to the Jews (Gal. 2:1–2). Had Peter thought, given events in Caesarea, that he might be afforded the title "Apostle to the Gentiles"? Perhaps. Luke records this visit of Saul to Jerusalem in Acts 11:27–30, where he mentions Agabus' prediction of a great famine and the determination of the church in Jerusalem to send relief to those living in Judea, "sending it to the elders by the hand of Barnabas and Saul" (v. 30).

During this second visit to Jerusalem, Saul took with him Titus, a gentile convert, who was not circumcised (Gal. 2:1, 3). It was imperative for Saul that circumcision not be seen as a necessary requirement of his justification. That would undo the very fabric of the gospel.

But trouble was brewing. "False brothers" had entered the discourse, spies for those for whom circumcision was essential (Gal. 2:4). For Paul, this was a gospel issue. Are we saved by faith *alone*, apart from the works of the law (Rom. 3:28; 4:6)? Or are we saved by faith *plus* adherence to Jewish boundary markers such as circumcision and kosher-food laws? The answer to these questions needed to be absolutely clear.

It was on this occasion that Saul encountered Peter again. He acknowledged that God had worked "through Peter for his apostolic ministry to the circumcised" (Gal. 2:8). He also acknowledged that Cephas (Peter), James (the Lord's brother, rather than John's brother), and John "seemed to be pillars" of the Jerusalem church and that they had given him and Barnabas "the right hand of fellowship" (v. 9).

Table Manners

Sometime later, Peter came to Antioch, where Saul was also present. Things seemed to be going well. The Antioch church was largely gentile, and Peter got along well with them, eating and fellowshipping with them. But then "certain men ... from James" came into town with intentions to spy out what was going on (Gal. 2:12). Rumors circulated in Jerusalem that Peter and the others were now openly eating with gentiles, eating forbidden food, and fellowshipping with those who were uncircumcised as if the matter was of no consequence.

When these men of James arrived, Peter did a complete reversal. He turned his back on the gentile brothers and sat at table with the circumcised Jewish brothers. The tension was electrifying. The Jewish believers saw it. The gentile brothers saw it. And Saul saw it. And he was mad as a hornet. Peter's actions were not only rude; they were in effect a complete denial of the free grace of the gospel. Even if cowardice drove him to do this (Paul in Galatians writes of Peter's "fearing the circumcision party"; 2:12), his actions were saying, loudly and clearly, that unless you comply with Jewish boundary markers, you are not truly saved. For Saul, this was a line too far. Peter had to be confronted, quickly, decisively, and publicly.

This was no time for a private, behind-closed-doors talk. Everyone in the room needed a primer on gospel dynamics, or else the future of the church would be in jeopardy. Refusing to eat with gentiles was much more than a racial slur; it was a denial of the gospel itself. Peter's actions (and it is a mark of how powerful he had become) affected the rest of the Jewish believers present, and even Barnabas, one of the most cherished believers in the New Testament, sided with Peter and refused to sit with the gentiles in the room. Their actions constituted hypocrisy (Gal. 2:13). They were "not in step with the truth of the gospel," and Saul spoke to Peter in the hearing of them all: "If you, though a Jew, live like a Gentile and not like a Jew, how can you force the Gentiles to live like Jews?" (v. 14).

Saul "opposed [Peter] to his face" (v. 11). I suspect that you could have heard the proverbial pin drop at that moment. The fact that Paul records it in Galatians, several years after the event, a letter that Peter undoubtedly read, is a testimony to just how damning an issue Peter and his friends caused that day in Antioch. Fear of offending James led Peter to an action that, in effect, denied the gospel itself.

Actions have consequences, and some actions have considerable consequences. Fear, Peter's besetting sin, had gotten the better of him again. Peter was prepared to sever friendships, risk embarrassing himself and others, and jeopardize the message of justification rather than conquer his fear. At this moment, he feared the leaders in the church at Jerusalem more than he feared

God. It would be a lesson that he would recall later when he urged his readers to "fear God" (1 Peter 2:17).

The Doctrine of Justification

Martin Luther famously pronounced the Protestant doctrine of justification as the article on which the church stands or falls. If we lose it, we lose Christianity. John Calvin echoed the same sentiment, writing in his *Institutes of the Christian Religion* that justification is "the main hinge on which religion turns."[4]

For Saul (Paul—and Peter knew this too), Peter's actions had introduced into the dining room the heresy of the "damnable plus." Are we justified by faith alone, apart from works, or are we justified by faith *plus* works? As Paul astutely recognized, to suggest that gentiles need to be circumcised and to obey kosher-food laws means that justification requires obedience to the law on our part.

- Faith *plus* circumcision
- Faith *plus* compliance with food laws

This is not a message of free grace.
It is not *good news*.
It is a message of grace *plus* works on my part.
It is a message of the "damnable plus."

Peter should have been singing these lines:

Nothing in my hand I bring,
simply to thy cross I cling;
naked, come to thee for dress;
helpless, look to thee for grace;
foul, I to the Fountain fly;
wash me, Savior, or I die.[5]

Instead, Peter was, in effect, singing,

Something in my hands I bring,
also, to thy cross I cling;
clothed, come to thee for dress,

looking to thee for additional grace;

foul-ish, I to the Fountain fly;

together, we wash, or else I die.

The poem has poor rhythm, and so does its theology. It is a doctrine of works-based justification that will damn us all. And Paul was insistent: "We know that a person is not justified by works of the law but through faith in Jesus Christ, so we also have believed in Christ Jesus, in order to be justified by faith in Christ and not by works of the law, because by works of the law no one will be justified" (Gal. 2:16). Peter was building up what he had torn down (cf. v. 18). He had put aside what he knew to be true in Joppa and Caesarea. He had listened to the voice of the evil one, who knew which buttons to push. The fear of man had replaced the fear of God.

Standing Firm

When Peter wrote his first epistle, he commended the "true grace of God" to his readers, adding, "Stand firm in it" (1 Peter 5:12).

The doctrine of justification by faith alone, apart from the works of the law, was a rallying cry in the sixteenth-century Reformation. The Genevan-Italian Reformed theologian Francis Turretin (1623–87) wrote of the pastoral relevance of justification by faith:

> Here then is the true state of the controversy. When the mind is thoroughly terrified with the consciousness of sin and a sense of God's wrath, what is that thing on account of which he may be acquitted before God and be reckoned a righteous person? What is that righteousness which he ought to oppose to the judgment of God that he may not be condemned according to the strict demands of the law (*akribodikaion*), but may obtain remission of sins and a right to eternal life? Is it righteousness inhering in us and inchoate holiness or the righteousness and obedience of Christ alone imputed to us? Our opponents hold the former; we the latter.[6]

It is not belief in the doctrine of justification that saves. It is faith in Christ that saves us. But we grasp Him by faith as an instrument, a faith that is itself a gift, "not a result of works, so that no one may boast" (Eph. 2:8–9).

That day in Antioch, Peter would have affirmed every word of the true gospel. He wasn't about to go rogue and deny the way of salvation so carefully taught to him by Jesus Himself. But he was afraid of being on the wrong side of people he thought important. Perhaps he thought his future looked better if he sided with James. For now, at least, James was more important than Paul. Paul was yet to make his mark. He had not yet engaged in a single missionary journey. Nor had he planted a single church or written a single letter. Paul's significance would rise and overshadow that of Peter and James. But that was later, and for now at least, Peter must side with the people that matter. And he did—to his great shame. He brought division and confusion in doing so and an encounter with Paul that neither would ever forget. And Paul made sure that we don't forget it, either. For Paul to relate the incident so graphically was not out of spite; it was to ensure that the purity of the gospel, with its central doctrine of justification by faith alone, be maintained.

We are all capable of buckling under the pressure of influencers. People can matter more to us than principles. For everyone from teenagers to mature believers like Peter, standing with those that matter can sometimes seem more important than standing, perhaps alone, on the side of truth. It wasn't just pork that might have been on the table. The eternal salvation of men and women was also on the table, and Peter should have known that. I think he did, but he bowed to the pressure of the men of James and paid the price: a public, stinging rebuke from Paul.

Peter had an Achilles' heel: his fear of man.

19

Prison Time, Again

After the disastrous visit to Antioch, Peter made his way back to Jerusalem, probably with the men of James with whom he had sided. The sting of Paul's rebuke was still fresh in his memory. But Jerusalem would see Peter in more trouble, this time from Herod Agrippa I.

Tertullian (c. AD 155–220), the second/third-century apologist for Christianity from North Africa, wrote in his *Apologeticus* that "the blood of the martyrs is the seed of the church."[1] You might think that after the violent death of Stephen, the church would be wary of provoking the wrath of the governing authorities and go underground. But the opposite is the case. The Jesus movement spread northward and grew. It was no longer a mere sect of Judaism; it was an entity in its own right, and Luke has been referring to "the church" for some time (Acts 5:11; 8:1, 3; 9:31; 11:22, 26; 12:1).

Evidently, King Herod[2] was alarmed by the growth and the threat that Christianity posed to the stability of his realm. The death of James—the brother of John, one of the Sons of Thunder—was a massive blow. Luke records the incident as being done "with the sword" (that is, a beheading) and identifies the reason: "Herod the king laid violent hands on some who belonged to the church. He killed James the brother of John with the sword" (12:1–2).

The execution "pleased the Jews," and Herod also had Peter arrested (v. 3). It was Passover time, and the city was full of people celebrating the days of Unleavened Bread. Herod wanted to put on a display of strength and rid Jerusalem of the scourge of this Jesus movement. In prison, probably in the Antonia

123

Fortress adjacent to the temple, Peter was guarded by "four squads" (Greek, *tetradiois*, meaning "foursome") of soldiers (v. 4), and he was "bound with two chains" (v. 6). Sixteen soldiers to guard one person seems heavy-handed, but Peter had managed to escape in the past, and news of it was probably still fresh in Herod's memory (5:19).

Why was Peter's "trial" delayed until "after the Passover" (12:4)? We are not told. Perhaps it had something to do with an impending Sabbath. Perhaps it had to do with an act of clemency that occurred at Passover. At Passover, Pilate had offered to release a prisoner as an attempt to rescue Jesus by comparing Him to the insurrectionist Barabbas (Mark 15:6–15). But more likely is the fact that an execution during Passover would appear unseemly.

What would you do if you thought you might be executed within a few days? Peter, chained to two soldiers on either side, decided to sleep (Acts 12:6). And to sleep so soundly that the angelic night visitor who entered the cell had to strike him on the side to wake him up (v. 7). It takes very little to rob some of us of sleep, but Peter evidently found such courage and strength that even an uncomfortable cell, two soldiers, and an impending trial and death sentence could not keep him awake. Peter cast his anxieties on Jesus in the certainty that Jesus cared for him (1 Peter 5:7). It is a lesson that all of us need to learn.

As Peter stands up, his chains fall off. Apparently, the two soldiers remain asleep. Putting on his clothes and sandals, Peter is instructed by the angel to disguise himself by wrapping his cloak around him and to follow his night visitor out of the cell (Acts 12:8). Luke tells us that Peter thought he was dreaming (v. 9).

Passing the first and second guards, they came to the iron gate that led to the city. The gate opened "of its own accord," and as soon as Peter was outside in the street, the angel left him (v. 10). Realizing that this was not a dream, he made his way to the house of Mary and her son, John Mark[3] (v. 12). Mary's house may have been the one Jesus used on the eve of His death, and now it has become a place where many had gathered to pray for Peter.

Peter's escape was an act of supernatural power. It was an intervention by God in space and time to radically change Peter's circumstances. He had been doomed to die at the hands of a brutal king and the growing hatred of the Sanhedrin, but God intervened. The circumstances had seemed inevitable, but

God changed them. God did the impossible. Though Peter had experienced a prison break before, he was not expecting a repeat performance. Yet Peter was in the hands of a sovereign, omnipotent God.

Corporate Prayer

What were the rest of the disciples in Jerusalem doing while Peter was awaiting his trial? Some of them came together to pray (Acts 12:12). There was only one way that this situation could change: God's supernatural intervention to change Herod's heart. And so they prayed, earnestly and faithfully, asking the Lord to hear them and answer their prayers.

It is an example of the power of corporate prayer. Though, as we will see, they were not expecting the Lord to answer their prayer so quickly and so dramatically, nevertheless their prayer evoked a response in the heart of God, and an angel was dispatched to go and get Peter out from his prison cell.

Prayer changes things. More accurately, God changes things. But He often accomplishes His purposes through the prayers of His people. He calls us to "watch and pray" (Matt. 26:41). And the Scriptures exhort us to "pray without ceasing" (1 Thess. 5:17).

Luke describes the prayers of the disciples as "earnest" (Acts 12:5), and he does so in a way that suggests that Peter was in prison for several days. In a sermon on this passage in Acts, C.H. Spurgeon notes the following:

As soon as Herod had put Peter into prison the church began to pray. Herod took care that the guards should be sufficient in number to keep good watch over his victim, but the saints of God set their watches too. As in times of war, when two armies lie near each other they both set their sentries, so in this case Herod had his sentries of the night keep watch, and the church had its pickets too. Prayer was made of the church without ceasing: as soon as one little company were compelled to separate to go to their daily labour, they were relieved by another company, and when some were forced to take rest in sleep, others were ready to take up the blessed work of supplication. Thus both sides were on the alert, and the guards were changed both by day and night. It was not hard to foresee which side would win the victory, for truly unless the Lord keep the city the watchmen waketh but in vain; and when, instead of helping to keep the castle, God sends angels to open doors and gates, then we may be sure that the watchmen will wake in vain, or fall into a dead slumber. Continually, therefore, the people of God pleaded at his mercy-seat; relays of petitioners appeared before the throne. Some mercies are not given except in answer to importunate prayer. There are blessings which, like ripe fruit, drop into your hand the moment you touch the bough; but there are others which require you to shake the tree again and again, until you make it rock with the vehemence of your exercise, for then only will the fruit fall down. My brethren, we must cultivate importunity in prayer. While the sun is shining and when the sun has gone down, still should prayer be kept up and fed with fresh fuel, so that it burns fiercely, and flames on high like a beacon fire blazing towards heaven.[4]

These words are worth pondering. Much is lost by a lack of earnest corporate prayer.

Knock, Knock!

The narrative of what happened next has something of an amusing twist to it. Surely Luke knew this when he described the incident. Peter's friends have gathered to pray for him. It is the middle of the night, and they cannot sleep. James has been killed, and Peter seems to be next. How could they survive without Peter? What would they do? Suddenly, there's a knock at the door. Is it a squad of soldiers sent by Herod? Is this a troop of temple guards coming to arrest them?

A servant girl named Rhoda goes to the door that leads to the street and hears Peter outside. Filled with joy, she runs inside to tell the others, leaving Peter in the street. The disciples do not believe her and accuse her of being "out of [her] mind" (Acts 12:14–15). Knowing that *someone* was outside, they suggest that it is Peter's "angel," a reference to a somewhat superstitious belief in late Judaism that there were guardian angels that looked like them (v. 15).

It is worth noting that the very thing that they were praying for had happened, and yet they did not believe it. Their prayers were mingled with doubt. They could not bring themselves to believe that what they prayed for could happen. It is a weakness that betrays us all. "All things are possible for one who believes," Jesus said, to which one responded, "I believe; help my unbelief!" (Mark 9:23–24).

The faith of the disciples gathered in Mary's home was earnest but weak. It was faith mingled with doubt. And Luke tells of it in a manner that brings a sense of humor, that laughs, not at the disciples, but at us, because we see in their response something that is all too familiar to us. We, too, have been guilty of weak prayer. We pray for the eradication of cancer but doubt that someone so ill can ever truly recover. We succumb to the "not my will, but yours, be done" mentality, yielding to what we think is inevitable and baptizing our unbelief with a resignation to divine sovereignty. Unlike Jacob, when the pain is too intense to bear, we fail to say, "I will not let you go unless you bless me" (Gen. 32:26). We must heed the words of Jesus: "Have faith in God. Truly, I say to you, whoever says to this mountain, 'Be taken up and thrown into the sea,' and does not doubt in his heart, but believes that what he says will come to pass, it will be done for him. Therefore I tell you, whatever you ask in prayer, believe that you have received it, and it will be yours" (Mark 11:22–24).

Another Place

When Peter was eventually brought inside, after continuing to knock on the door, the disciples heard Peter's story of the angel who sprang him from prison. They must have been in awe of the power of God.

But there was a price on Peter's head. It was too dangerous for him to remain in Jerusalem, and having asked them to report his miraculous release to James (the Lord's brother) and the other disciples in the city, Peter "went to another place" (Acts 12:17). Meanwhile, in the morning, Herod had the sentries executed. Then Herod left for Caesarea. According to ancient historians, Herod, wearing a robe woven with silver thread, put on games in honor of Caesar. It is said that the people cried out before him, "The voice of a god, and not of a man!" (v. 22). Five days later the god was dead, eaten by worms (vv. 20–23).

Where did Peter go? We do not know. He makes one more appearance in Acts, at the gathering of the elders at the Jerusalem council in chapter 15. Herod was dead, and it wasn't safe for Peter to return to Jerusalem. This occurred around AD 50.

Paul was there, as was Barnabas. And Paul had much to say. Peter was probably still smarting from the Antioch refutation, but he rose to the occasion and spoke powerfully, leading the council to conclude that gentiles did not need to observe Mosaic ceremonial laws such as circumcision and the dietary restrictions. The only exception was "that [they] abstain from what has been sacrificed to idols, and from blood, and from what has been strangled, and from sexual immorality"[5] (15:29).

Peter made a compelling case for gentile inclusion, arguing that he had been set apart (at Joppa) and that through his mouth the gentiles would hear the word of the gospel and believe (v. 7). He pushed back on those who were "putting God to the test" by putting "a yoke on the neck of the disciples that neither [their] fathers nor [they] have been able to bear" (v. 10). He was referring to the inference that gentiles would need to come to Jerusalem to celebrate Jewish festivals. For Jews such as Peter, who lived far away from Jerusalem, attending the feasts (involving a pilgrimage to Jerusalem and several days away from family and work) was a considerable burden. For gentiles, who lived even farther away, the burden would be even greater.

Peter also drew attention to the way that gentiles at Caesarea had received the Holy Spirit, just as the Jews had done in Jerusalem. The gentiles, too, would be saved "through the grace of the Lord Jesus" (v. 11).

From this point forward, Peter disappears into the background. Paul will now take center stage. Where did Peter go? From this point until he appears in Rome at the time of his execution, fifteen or sixteen years pass. That is a long time to be in the background. He would have been in his fifties or early sixties.

There are conjectures that he went to Rome.[6] Peter writes to the "elect exiles of the Dispersion in Pontus, Galatia, Cappadocia, Asia, and Bithynia," suggesting that he had some connection with the churches in Asia Minor (1 Peter 1:1). James now seems to be the chief Apostle in Jerusalem, and Luke will now focus on Paul's missionary labors.

Peter seems to have been taken out of the limelight. God had something quieter for him to do. It must have been difficult for him to assume this seemingly lesser role.

Perhaps Peter and Paul's relationship never completely healed after Antioch.[7] Given that Paul records the incident in such agonizing detail, it must have been difficult for Peter to read.[8]

There are also suggestions in 1 Corinthians that Peter was at Corinth for a time. The Corinthian church was known for its factionalism. Significantly, there was even a "Cephas" following (1 Cor. 1:12). It is interesting to note that there are four references to Peter in 1 Corinthians, and in every instance, Paul uses his Aramaic name, Cephas, rather than his Greek name, Peter (1:12; 3:22; 9:5; 15:5). Does this suggest, as one writer thinks, that the name Cephas "identifies Peter with the earliest, and thus, perhaps, in the minds of the Corinthians, the most authentic version of the faith, having its roots in Jerusalem"?[9]

At some point, Peter wrote two epistles, showing his continuing pastoral care over the churches with which he was particularly familiar.[10] And we know that Peter eventually made it to Rome.

Peter's Death

There remain accounts that Peter witnessed the execution of his wife in Rome. Clement of Alexandria, a bishop in the late first century, describes the scene:

> So we are told that the blessed Peter, when he beheld his wife on her way to execution, rejoiced on account of her call and her homeward journey, and addressed her by name with words of exhortation and good cheer, bidding her "remember the Lord."[11]

There are also apocryphal accounts of Peter's children that Clement recounts.[12] We read of a daughter who had been lame from childhood and whom Peter refused to heal, lest she marry some rich man against the wishes of her parents. The claim is made that she had been seen bathing with her mother by a man called Ptolemy. What kept her from being defiled was her deformity, for which Peter gave thanks to the Lord.

These recollections may be fantasy, of course.

At the end of John's gospel, Jesus hinted at the manner of Peter's death (John 21:18–19).[13] According to tradition, Peter and Paul were arrested and imprisoned in Rome in AD 64, during the reign of Emperor Nero. It is unlikely that they were in the same cell. Both were executed (probably not at the same time): Paul (because he was a citizen) was beheaded, and Peter (who was not a citizen) was crucified upside down. Peter's execution is believed to have been in AD 64.[14]

Peter's death is attested by Tertullian in his *Prescription against Heretics*, and according to Eusebius, Origen (AD 184–253) writes, "Peter was crucified at Rome with his head downwards, as he himself had desired to suffer."[15]

From fisherman to Apostle to martyr. So comes an end to Peter's extraordinary life. Despite his glaring faults, he was the "rock," a "pillar" of the church (Gal. 2:9).

God uses flawed people to accomplish His purpose.

We should not judge Peter too harshly, lest we forget that we, too, are jars of clay.

Notes

Chapter 1

1 See Richard Bauckham, *Jesus and the Eyewitnesses: The Gospels as Eyewitness Testimony* (Grand Rapids, Mich.: Eerdmans, 2017).

2 Christina Rossetti, "In the Bleak Midwinter" (1872).

3 Estimates range from the mid-50s to early 90s. D.A. Carson tentatively suggests AD 80. See D.A. Carson, *The Gospel according to John* (Leicester, England: Inter-Varsity Press; Grand Rapids, Mich.: Eerdmans, 1991), 82.

Chapter 2

1 David F. Wells, *God in the Wasteland* (Grand Rapids, Mich.: Eerdmans, 1994), 88.

2 The Greek translated "believing wife" is literally "sister as wife," and Roman Catholic interpreters put the stress on "sister" and suggest that the word "wife" means something else.

3 The lake was known by various names at this time, including the Sea of Galilee and the Sea of Tiberias.

4 See John 1:41, where Andrew refers to Jesus as "Messiah."

5 Cecil Frances Alexander, "Jesus Calls Us" (1852).

Chapter 3

1 Greek, *protos*.

2 William Cowper, "God Moves in a Mysterious Way" (1774).

3 See Luke 3:21–22; Mark 1:35–36; Luke 5:15–16; Luke 6:12–13; John 6:11; Mark 7:31–37; Matt. 15:36; Luke 9:18; Luke 9:28–29; Luke 10:17–21; Luke 11:1; John 11:41–42; Matt. 19:13–15; Luke 22:17; Luke 22:31–32; John 17:1–26; Matt. 26:36–46; Luke 23:34; Matt. 27:46; Luke 23:46; Luke 24:30.

4 C.S. Lewis, *The Screwtape Letters* (1942; repr., New York: HarperCollins, 1996), 45–46.

Chapter 4

1 A similar (but fictitious) tale is often repeated about Julius Caesar's landing on the shores of Britannica on August 25, 55 BC. There is no evidence that he burned his ships, forcing his men to stay and fight. In fact, he returned to Gaul shortly thereafter.

2 The transubstantiation view understands, *in some sense or other*, a literal transformation of the bread and wine into the physical body and blood of Christ. While the average Roman Catholic might conceive of this literally, Roman Catholic theologians distinguish between form and substance and argue that the bread and wine still appear as such to the taste but that in reality, which cannot be seen or tasted, they are the body and blood of Christ.

3   E.g., F.F. Bruce, *The Hard Sayings of Jesus* (Downers Grove, Ill.: IVP Academic, 1983); Steve Timmis, *I Wish Jesus Hadn't Said That* (Grand Rapids, Mich.: Zondervan, 2014); Lloyd Ogilvie, *Understanding the Hard Sayings of Jesus* (Dallas: Word, 1989).

4   Horatius Bonar, "I Heard the Voice of Jesus Say" (1846).

Chapter 5

1   The city may also be the one known as Baal-gad (Josh. 11:17; 12:7; 13:5), literally "Master Luck," the god of fortune, and later associated with Pan.

2   The State of Theology, https://thestateoftheology.com.

3   Barbara Thiering, *Jesus & the Riddle of the Dead Sea Scrolls: Unlocking the Secrets of His Life Story* (San Francisco: HarperSanFrancisco), 1992.

Chapter 6

1   WCF 8.5 (emphasis added).

2   Q&A 12.

3   Horatius Bonar, "Go, Labor On" (1843).

4   John Calvin, *A Little Book on the Christian Life*, eds. and trans. Aaron C. Denlinger and Burk Parsons (Orlando, Fla.: Ligonier Ministries, 2017), 81–82.

5   Dietrich Bonhoeffer, *The Cost of Discipleship* (1948; repr., London: SCM, 2001), 44.

Chapter 7

1   The transfiguration is recorded in all three Synoptic Gospels (Matt. 17:1–13; Mark 9:2–13; Luke 9:28–36). Matthew and Mark specifically say that *six* days have passed (Matt. 17:1; Mark 9:2), but Luke has a more general statement: "About eight days after these sayings" (Luke 9:28). Perhaps Luke included both the promise Jesus made to the disciples that they would not taste death until they had seen His kingdom (Luke 9:27) and the day of the transfiguration itself. In any case, "about" signals an approximation, not a precise timeline.

2   Others have suggested Mount Hermon.

Chapter 8

1   For a fuller account, see Ryan Reiterman, "Arnie: Palmer and the agony of defeat(s)," The Golf Channel, September 10, 2014, accessed June 6, 2022, https://www.golfchannel.com/news/arnie-arnold-palmer-and-agony-defeat.

2   Harmonizing these predictions is notoriously difficult, and what I have written here is simply my attempt at doing so.

3   Jonathan Edwards, *Thoughts on the New England Revival: Vindicating the Great Awakening* (Edinburgh, Scotland: Banner of Truth, 2005), 156–73.

4   John Murray, "The Heavenly, Priestly Activity of Christ," in *Collected Works of John Murray*, vol. 1, *The Claims of Truth* (Edinburgh, Scotland: Banner of Truth, 1976), 48.

5   James Montgomery, "In the Hour of Trial" (1834).

Chapter 9

1   D.A. Carson, *The Gospel according to John* (Leicester, England: Inter-Varsity Press; Grand Rapids, Mich.: Eerdmans, 1991), 578.

2   Harmonizing the accounts of Peter's denial is famously difficult, and the approach taken here is simply one attempt at doing so.

3 Matthew has Peter "sitting" and John has him "standing" at this point. The variations in the accounts are considerable. Nevertheless, there is little sense of time in these accounts, and it is more than likely that several hours have passed and that Peter, nervous and fearful, would both stand and sit.

4 Matthew has Peter saying at this point, "I do not know what you mean" (Matt. 26:70). The so-called discrepancies in the four accounts of Peter's denial led Harold Lindsell to abandon all hope of reconciliation, suggesting that there were *six* denials! See Harold Lindsell, *Battle for the Bible* (Grand Rapids, Mich.: Zondervan, 1976), 174–76. But in a world where accounts were initially oral, without the use of quotation marks that we are so used to, the essence of what Peter said is maintained, and the essential *meaning* is precisely the same. For more on this issue, see Craig Blomberg, *Historical Reliability of the Gospels* (Downers Grove, Ill.: IVP Academic, 2007).

5 Luke employs the more generic masculine form (*heteros*), not clearly specifying a gender, and John employs *eipon* ("they said"; John 18:25), suggesting that others concurred with the accusation of the servant girl. Mark calls her *hē paidiskē*, "one of the servant girls" (Mark 14:66). Some translations have "*the* servant girl," suggesting the same servant girl as in the first denial. But this translation is not grammatically necessary.

6 Luke has only one person in his account (*allos*; Luke 22:59), and John specifically calls him a servant of the high priest (John 18:26). This happens often in the Gospels. Sometimes in one account there are two people to whom Jesus ministers, but only one of them speaks, so one gospel will simply mention the one who speaks. Also, Mark has an observation that others might have agreed with the servant of the high priest (whom he does not mention), with "the bystanders" saying, "Certainly you are one of them, for you are a Galilean" (Mark 14:70).

7 As we suggested in the previous chapter, to harmonize the crowing after the third denial with Mark's account (Peter's account), this crowing was not the first one; the rooster had *also* crowed after the first denial (Mark 14:68).

Chapter 10

1 Matthew says that it was "toward the dawn," perhaps indicating that by the time Mary got to the tomb, the sun had begun to rise (Matt. 28:1).

2 Joseph Hart, "Come, Ye Sinners, Poor and Wretched" (1759).

Chapter 11

1 Derek W.H. Thomas, *Heaven on Earth: What the Bible Teaches about Life to Come* (Fearn, Scotland: Christian Focus, 2018), 89.

2 For the mathematically curious, Archimedes, in his *Measurement of a Circle*, referred to the ratio (153/265) as constituting the "measure of the fish," this ratio being an imperfect representation of $1/\sqrt{3}$.

3 Gematria is a Jewish form of numerology in which the letters of the Hebrew alphabet are substituted with corresponding numbers.

4 See William Hendriksen, *John* (Edinburgh, Scotland: Banner of Truth, 1959), 487.

5 See D.A. Carson, *The Gospel according to John* (Leicester, England: Inter-Varsity Press; Grand Rapids, Mich.: Eerdmans, 1991), 676.

Chapter 12

1 The ESV has "as far as Bethany," but it could also be "in the vicinity of Bethany."
2 John Calvin, *The Acts of the Apostles*, eds. David W. Torrance and Thomas F. Torrance (Grand Rapids, Mich.: Eerdmans, 1966), 1:29.
3 See David G. Peterson, *The Acts of the Apostles* (Grand Rapids, Mich.: Eerdmans; Cambridge, England: Apollos, 2009), 109.
4 "Pentecost" in Greek means "fiftieth"; the festival, also known as the Feast of Weeks, comes fifty days after Passover.
5 The miracle was one of speaking rather than hearing.
6 Taking the first letter of each division, these three sections were called the Tanakh.
7 Most scholars date Joel *after* the exile in 586 BC.

Chapter 13

1 Some see a reference to the Lord's Supper in the words "breaking of bread" (cf. Acts 2:46, where a reference is made to "breaking bread in their homes"). But this is unlikely, and my own view is that this is a reference to ordinary meals shared together for the purposes of fellowship.
2 Note that Luke includes the definite article, "*the* prayers."
3 The Beautiful Gate (Acts 3:2, 10) is not mentioned in other historical sources. Multiple suggestions have been made, and it is likely that this is a reference to one of the outer gates.
4 "'Dr. Motyer concluded' by Timothy Keller, *Tolle Lege* (blog), August 26, 2016, accessed June 10, 2022, https://tollelege.net/2016/08/26/dr-motyer-concluded -by-timothy-keller.
5 Cecil Frances Alexander, "There Is a Green Hill Far Away" (1848).
6 The ESV translates it as "founder and perfecter."
7 Charles Wesley, "Love Divine, All Loves Excelling" (1747).

Chapter 14

1 Alexander Solzhenitsyn, *The Gulag Archipelago* (New York: Harper & Row, 1973), 2:617.
2 Rob Bell, *Love Wins: A Book about Heaven, Hell, and the Fate of Every Person Who Ever Lived* (New York: HarperOne, 2012).
3 Brian McLaren, *A Generous Orthodoxy: Why I Am a Missional, Evangelical, Post/Protestant, Liberal/Conservative, Mystical/Poetic, Biblical, Charismatic/ Contemplative, . . . Emergent, Unfinished Christian* (Grand Rapids, Mich.: Zondervan, 2006).
4 The term was first used by the Roman Catholic theologian Karl Rahner.

Chapter 15

1 John Chrysostom, *Saint Chrysostom's Homilies on the Acts of the Apostles and the Epistle to the Romans*, ed. Philip Schaff, Nicene and Post-Nicene Fathers of the Christian Church 11 (Whitefish, Mont.: Kessinger, 2004), 73.
2 It is possible that "public prison" should be translated "in prison publicly." This would suggest that the arrest was done in a public manner as a deterrent to the growing number of Jesus-followers in the city.
3 Quoted in G. Holden Pike, *Life and Work of Charles Haddon Spurgeon* (Edinburgh, Scotland: Banner of Truth, 1991), 2:352.

Chapter 16

1 "The Aramaic name *Tabitha* and the Greek name *Dorcas* both mean *gazelle*" (ESV footnote).

2 Edward Perronet, "All Hail the Power of Jesus' Name!" (1779).

Chapter 17

1 The Nicene Creed (AD 325).

2 J. Gresham Machen, *Christianity and Liberalism* (Grand Rapids, Mich.: Eerdmans, 2009), 135.

Chapter 18

1 There are two movies by this title: a 2010 remake and the 1981 original. There are differences in the stories, but they both involve a rivalry between Olympians that threatens the destruction of the Greek city of Argos by the Kraken, the last Titan. Perseus, the demigod son of Zeus, must go on a journey to prevent the catastrophe.

2 Acts 11 does not indicate how much time elapsed after Peter's defense in Jerusalem and his visit to Antioch or what he was doing in between these occasions. Nor does Luke relate the clash between Peter and Paul in Antioch. The fact that the issue of circumcision as a requirement for gentiles is being discussed in Galatians means that the epistle must have been written *before* the Jerusalem council in Acts 15 where this issue was settled once and for all.

3 Saul is first called "Paul" in Acts 13:9, on the island of Cyprus. Saul is his Hebrew name and Paul his Roman name. It made it easier for Saul to go by his Roman name when ministering to gentiles.

4 John Calvin, *Institutes of the Christian Religion*, 3.11.1.

5 Augustus M. Toplady, "Rock of Ages, Cleft for Me" (1776).

6 Francis Turretin, *Institutes of Elenctic Theology*, ed. J.T. Dennison, trans. G.M. Giger (Phillipsburg, N.J.: P&R, 1992–97), 2:640.

Chapter 19

1 Tertullian, *Apologeticus*, l.13.

2 There are several rulers named Herod in the New Testament, and the one mentioned in Acts 12 is Herod Agrippa I, king of Judea from AD 41 to 44, the grandson of Herod the Great, the ruler who tried to kill Jesus when he authorized a pogrom against infant boys up to age two in Bethlehem, and the nephew of Herod Antipas, the ruler in Galilee.

3 John Mark is the author of the gospel of Mark, companion of Barnabas and Paul, who accompanied them on their missionary travels (Acts 12:25). He is also Barnabas' cousin (Col. 4:10).

4 Charles Haddon Spurgeon, "A Special Prayer Meeting," in *Metropolitan Tabernacle Pulpit*, vol. 21 (Pasadena, Tex.: Pilgrim, 1971), 437.

5 The reference to sexual immorality appears redundant, but it is possible that it is a reference to "the laws of consanguinity," the marriage of close relatives, as in the case of Herod Antipas and his brother's wife, Herodias (Mark 6:17), the cause of John the Baptist's death.

6 John Wenham, *Redating Matthew, Mark and Luke* (Eugene, Ore.: Wipf & Stock, 2020), 148.

7   See Martin Hengel, *Saint Peter: The Underestimated Apostle*, trans. Thomas H. Trapp (Grand Rapids, Mich.: Eerdmans, 2010), 96.

8   Since Galatians must have been written *before* the Jerusalem council, which met in AD 47/48 (or else Paul would have cited its conclusions in the letter), Galatians was probably written in AD 46/47.

9   Larry R. Helyer, *The Life and Witness of Peter* (Downers Grove, Ill.: IVP Academic/ Nottingham, England: Apollos, 2012), 98.

10   Conservatives date 1 Peter around AD 62/63 and 2 Peter shortly before the Apostle's death in AD 64.

11   Clement of Alexandria, *The Stromata* (*Miscellanies*), 7.63.3, trans. J.E.L. Oulton and H. Chadwick, Library of Christian Classics (Louisville, Ky.: Westminster John Knox, 1977), 133.

12   Clement, *Stromata*, 3.52.1–2; 3.52.5.

13   See chapter 11.

14   Some scholars give a range from AD 64 to 68.

15   Eusebius, *Church History*, 3.1, quoted in Sandra Sweeny Silver, *Footprints in Parchment: Rome versus Christianity, 30–313 AD* (Bloomington, Ind.: Authorhouse, 2013), 13. The apocryphal *Acts of Peter*, written in the second century, also includes a testimony to this effect.

Scripture Index

About the Author

Dr. Derek W.H. Thomas is a Ligonier Ministries teaching fellow and Chancellor's Professor of Systematic and Pastoral Theology at Reformed Theological Seminary. He previously served as senior minister of the First Presbyterian Church in Columbia, S.C. He is author of many books, including *Heaven on Earth*, *Strength for the Weary*, and *Let Us Worship God*.